Pacific Coast Inshore Fishes
Fourth Edition (Revised)

by

Daniel W. Gotshall

SEA CHALLENGERS, INC.
4 Sommerset Rise, Monterey, CA 93940

2001

A SEA CHALLENGERS PUBLICATION

Copy Editor: Hans Bertsch

Front Cover

Top photo:	Red Irish Lord, *Hemilepidotus hemilepidotus*
Center left photo:	Bluebanded Goby, *Lythrypnus dalli*
Center right photo:	Grunt Sculpin, *Rhamphocottus richardsonii*
Bottom photo:	Rainbow Scorpionfish, *Scorpaenodes xyris*

Photographs by Daniel W. Gotshall

Library of Congress Cataloging-in-Publication Data

Gotshall, Daniel.
   Pacific Coast Inshore Fishes / by Daniel W. Gotshall.--4th ed. rev.
   p.cm.
   Includes bibliographical references (p.).
   ISBN 0-930118-32-4
   1. Fishes--Pacific Coast (North America)--Identification. I. Title.
   QL623.4.G67 2001
   597.177'43--dc21   2001020289

SEA CHALLENGERS, INC.
4 Sommerset Rise, Monterey, CA 93940

Printed in Hong Kong through Global Interprint, Santa Rosa, CA, USA
Typography and Prepress Production by Diana Behrens, Danville, CA, USA

ACKNOWLEDGMENTS

This fourth edition is the product of many scientists and keen-eyed diver-naturalists. John McCosker and Douglas Long read portions of the manuscript and offered many corrections of my taxonomic errors. Robert Lea provided new taxonomic information on the sea basses, groupers, and ronquils, as well as confirming identifications of some of the sculpins.

Greg Jensen provided many of the new photographs of, and information on fishes that inhabit the soft bottoms of Puget Sound. Pat Collier, Jonathon Ramsay, Neil Mc Daniel, Sally Bartels, and Dave Wrobel reported new geographical and depth ranges. Brenda Irwin and Dave Thomas provided average length and catch data for canary rockfish.

Ann Gotshall made many corrections to the manuscript and entered it into the word processor. Hans Bertsch, as usual, did a fine job as copy editor.

This project could not have been completed without the assistance of all of these people. I thank them all for their generous time and energy.

PHOTO CREDITS

Photographer	Species Number
Lou Barr	29
Fred Bavendam	35, 175
Dan Blodgett	6
Ryan Borema	36, 106, 169, 171
Marc Chamberlain	9, 17, 93, 94, 163, 214
Marc Conlin	156
Cordell Expeditions	160
Steve Drogin	5
Phil Edgell	90
Eric D. Erikson	131
Bernie Hanby	78
Greg Jensen	28, 33, 40, 86, 87, 91, 100, 102, 103, 107, 109 111, 112, 114, 115, 117, 165, 167, 168, 170, 173, 176, 183, 201, 204, 205, 212
Neil Mc Daniel	27, 47, 82, 172
Kevin Mc Donnel	128
Chuck Tribolet	194
Visuals Unlimited/Glen M. Oliver	79

Drawings by Daniel J. Miller

TABLE OF CONTENTS

INTRODUCTION

As with the earlier editions of "Pacific Coast Inshore Fishes," this field guide is designed primarily for the use of divers, snorkelers and, to a certain extent, sport anglers. With the growing interest by scuba divers in observing and taking photographs rather than "harvesting" our near shore fishes, and with the increasing fishery regulations designed to conserve the dwindling populations of many of our near shore fishes, it is my hope that this field guide will assist all of you in identifying the fishes that you see.

This edition covers not only the common fishes encountered by most divers and snorkelers, in the area from Alaska to Central Baja California but also a new group of fishes that inhabit the soft bottoms formerly shunned by divers. During the last 10 or 12 years more and more divers are moving away from the reefs to explore the sandy and mud bottoms of our region. These "muck divers" encounter many species of fish not observed in rocky habitats. Night diving can be particularly rewarding, as many of these fishes stay hidden during daylight and only come out to forage after dark.

I have added about 45 species to this edition. Most are small fishes that spend most or all of their lives on or in soft bottoms. There are also several pelagic species new to this edition. These fishes are being encountered by divers who spend some hours around offshore "kelp rafts" that provide habitat for a number of immature and adult fishes.

Most of the fishes in this field guide spend at least part of their lives around reefs and kelp beds in depths shallower than 150 feet (45.5 m), and below the intertidal zone. Most of the species are fairly easy to identify underwater because of distinctive coloration, body shape or fin size and shape.

There are several references that I used in preparing this fourth edition; I particularly recommend the following for further information:

Pacific Coast Fishes by Eschmeyer, Herald and Hammann; *Pacific Fishes of Canada* by Hart; *Coastal Fishes of the Pacific Northwest* by Lamb and Edgell; and *Biological Aspects of Near Shore Rockfishes of the Genus* Sebastes by Lea, McAllister and Ventresca. These and several other recommended books are listed in the bibliography.

Conservation:

It is hard to believe, but over the past 40 years many populations of near shore fishes have declined to the point that some species are near "commercial extinction." That is, the populations can no longer support any type of economically viable fishing or harvesting. Included in this list are species that were once so common that many sport anglers considered them "trash" fish. The black rockfish certainly falls into this category. The brown, copper, widow, quillback, tiger, canary, yelloweye, and bocaccio rockfishes are also considered depleted or seriously threatened. Lingcod, one of the most sought after fish by bottom fish anglers is also considered depleted.

On the bright side, the giant sea bass population, which in California was considered close to extinction in the late 1970's, has increased to the point where divers once again encounter them commonly around all of the channel islands. This remarkable recovery, I am sure, is due to the complete closure of the sport and commercial fisheries for these fish in California.

Thus we know that at least some species will respond to complete protection. Size limits, decreased catch limits, and seasonal closures during spawning periods can also help some of these populations recover. However, in some cases, one or more of these management options would not work; for example, a size limit on many species of rockfish would not work because when some species are brought to the surface from the depths, the expansion of the gas bladder prevents successful release of undersize fish.

Marine scientists all along the Pacific Coast have been working on these problems for a long time, but because of the political pressure from sport and commercial fisheries, many of the recommendations for changes in management strategies have been rejected. One of the best management strategies that most marine scientists have recommended is the establishment of marine "no take" areas along the coast to protect the habitat and population of adults and juveniles of non-migratory species. These areas would be set aside permanently to allow each species to regain a population of spawners that could provide young fish to repopulate areas outside of the protected areas, thus acting as a natural hatchery.

What can you and I do to help bring back these populations? I suggest that we all begin by practicing non-intrusive, and non-extractive activities, particularly for those species that we know are threatened.

These include:
1. Follow the basic rule of "Take only pictures, leave only bubbles."
2. Foster a "Look, but do not touch" attitude toward all marine life.
3. Do not treat marine animals as "pets," i.e., do not pet, ride or feed!
4. Report all illegal activities.
5. When fishing, take only what you need and refrain from taking protected species.

How to Use Field Guides: The most effective way to use this or any other field guide is to review, review, review. By constantly going over the photographs, you will find that when diving it is common to look at an animal and remember having seen it in the guide. You may not remember the name, but you should be able quickly to locate the animal in question in your field guide. I also believe that by constant review, the shapes and colors of the animals become more familiar.

When using this guide, if an animal is unfamiliar, turn to the pictorial keys, page 7. Look for the shape that most closely resembles the animal you observed, then turn to that section and look at the photos. If your fish is not there, but you are convinced you have the right family, then you should consult other books or field guides (see Bibliography).

When looking at a fish you do not recognize, note in your mind or on a slate the general body shape; placement, shape and size of fins; color, particularly any spots, bars or stripes; and finally, in what type of habitat the fish was observed.

Common and Scientific Names:

The common and scientific names I have used in this guide are those recognized by the American Fisheries Society and are listed in their publication *Common and Scientific Names of Fishes from the United States and Canada* (see Bibliography).

New Information:

Many of the new range information came from reports by diver naturalists listed in the acknowledgments. I am always interested in hearing about new size records, northern or southern range extensions, and new depth records. If you encounter new data that do not appear in this guide, I would very much like to know about it. Please contact me at Sea Challengers, 4 Sommerset Rise, Monterey, CA 93940, or by e-mail at seachall@aol.com.

GLOSSARY

abdominal
In fish, assuming the pectoral fin is lying flat to the body, refers to the attachment of the pelvic fins between anus and middle of pectoral fins (See Figure 1).

adipose fin
An additional small, fleshy fin found on the midline near the tail in certain fishes such as the lizardfish; consists mostly of fatty tissue.

anterior
Of, toward, on, or near the front or head region of the fish's body.

barbel
Any of the slender, fleshy, whisker-like growths on the chin or lips of certain fishes such as the Pacific tomcod.

cirri (pl. of cirrus)
Fringelike skin flaps on top of the head (for example, see fringe-heads, pg.101) or other parts of the body.

canine teeth
Large, sharp, cone-shaped teeth used for grasping prey.

coronal spines
The head spine on certain rockfishes (Scorpaenidae) located at the rear of the bony ridge between the eyes.

cryptic
Hidden, tending to conceal or camouflage as "cryptic coloring;" tends to hide in caves or holes.

dorsal
Of, toward, on, in, or near the back of a fish or pertaining to the upper surface of the back.

fin membrane
Thin connective tissue found between the spines and rays of the fins of a fish.

gill arch
The curved bone located inside the gill cavity of bony fishes which supports the fish's gills; contains bony, toothlike structures on the forward edges called gill rakers.

gill rakers
The bony, toothlike projections on the forward edges of gill arches (see above) that function to protect the gills and strain food.

hermaphroditic
Possessing both male and female sex organs in one fish; sometimes, possessing first one set of sex organs and then the opposite sex organs sequentially in the same fish.

jugular
In fish, refers to the attachment of pelvic fins between rear edge of gill cover and rear of eye.

lateral line
A line of modified scales containing sensory pores that generally runs along the side of the fish from the back of the head to the tail fin.

mandible
The lower jaw; also the bone of the lower jaw.

maxillary
Pertains to the main bone of the animal's upper jaw. In some fish the maxillary, or jaw bone, may form the whole jaw, in others only the back portion of the jaw.

molar teeth
Broad, rounded teeth adapted for grinding and located toward the back of the mouth.

nape
Back of neck.

nocturnal	Describes fish that normally are inactive during the day and become active at night.
ocellus	A pigmented, usually ringed, eyelike spot; any spot on a fish resembling an eye.
opercular spine	Bony spines located on the rear edge of the gill cover.
oviparous	Reproduction by the release of eggs that are fertilized and hatch outside the body.
ovoviviparous	The type of reproduction in which fertilized eggs are retained, nurtured, and hatched *inside* the female. The eggs receive some nutrients and oxygen from the female, but do not develop a real placenta attaching them to the mother's body as in mammalian reproduction.
papillae (pl. of papilla)	Any small, soft, rounded, nipple-like projections or protuberances anywhere on a fish.
photophores	Specialized, well-defined, light-producing organs found in certain fishes; usually with a lens and round reflector.
posterior	Of, toward, on, in, or near the rear or tail region of the fish's body.
premaxillary	Refers to either of two bones located in front of maxillary bones.
preopercular spine	Any spines located on the rear edge of the preopercular bone (see Figure 1).
soft rays	The segmented and often branched soft bony spines that support the membranes of the fins of a fish.
spineous ray	A sharp, projecting fin ray that is neither segmented nor branched; usually rigid and helps support the membrane of the fins of a fish. Capable of causing injury.
suborbital stay	A usually thin bone located below the orbit of the eye and under the skin (see Figure 1).
symphyseal knob	The bony knob located beneath the tip of the lower jaw (see Figure 1), particularly on rockfish (Scorpaenidae).
thoracic	In fish, refers to the attachment of pelvic fins between middle of pectoral fins and the rear edge of the maxillary (see Figure 1).
ventral	Of, toward, on, in, or near the abdominal area, or pertaining to the lower or under surface of a fish.
viviparous	Method of reproduction in which living young (rather than eggs) are maintained inside the mother's body and nourished via a placenta until ready for birth, particularly in the Embiotocidae.

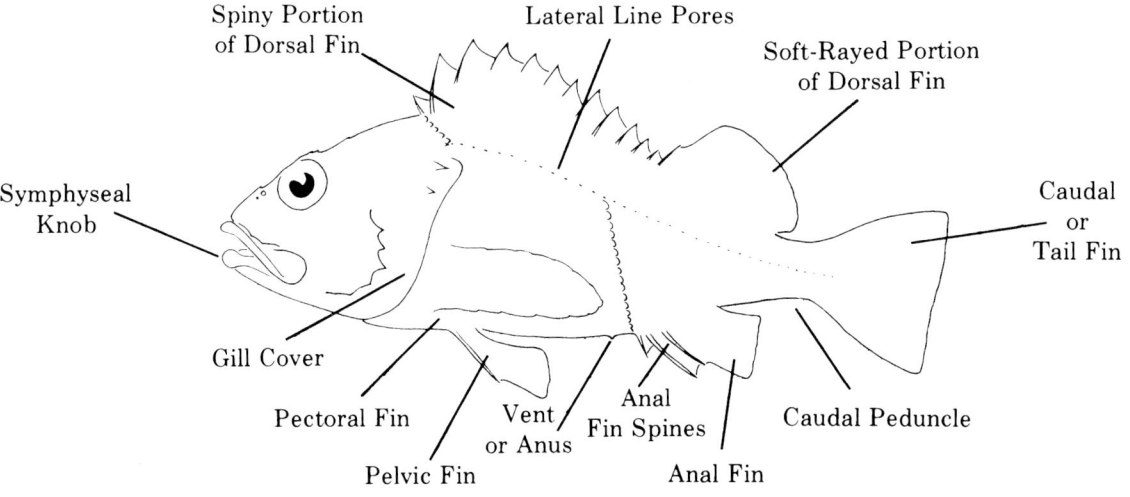

Spiny Portion
of Dorsal Fin

Lateral Line Pores

Soft-Rayed Portion
of Dorsal Fin

Symphyseal
Knob

Caudal
or
Tail Fin

Gill Cover

Pectoral Fin

Vent
or Anus

Pelvic Fin

Anal
Fin Spines

Caudal Peduncle

Anal Fin

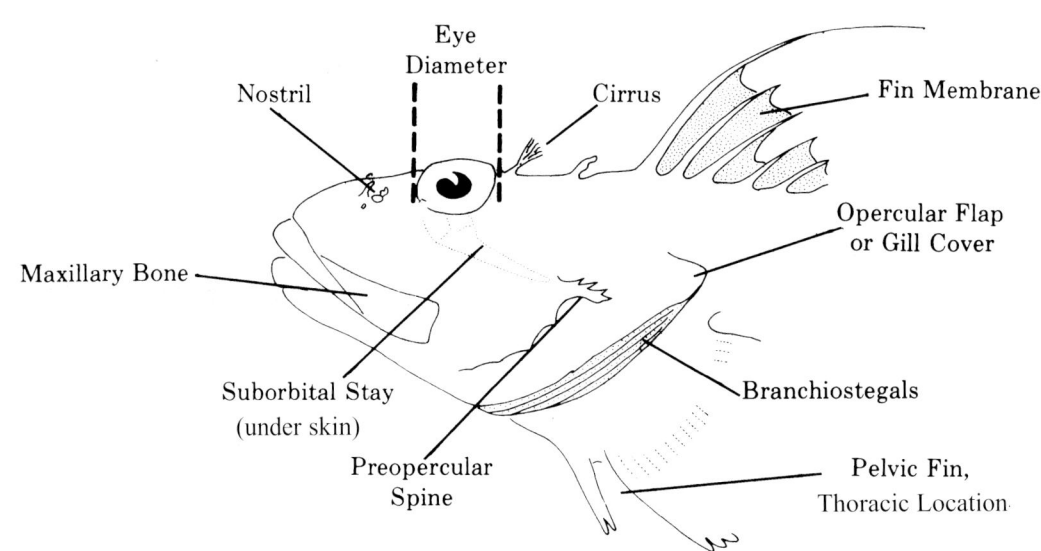

Eye
Diameter

Nostril

Cirrus

Fin Membrane

Maxillary Bone

Opercular Flap
or Gill Cover

Suborbital Stay
(under skin)

Branchiostegals

Preopercular
Spine

Pelvic Fin,
Thoracic Location

(Drawings by Daniel J. Miller)

Figure 1. Parts of a Bony Fish

PICTORIAL KEY TO FISH FAMILIES

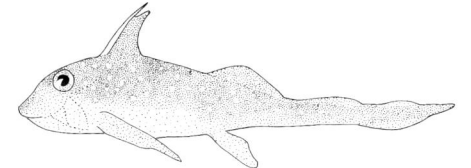

CHIMAERAS P. 16

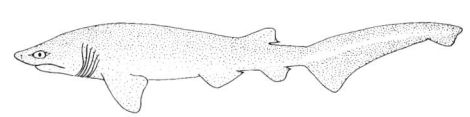

COW SHARKS P. 16

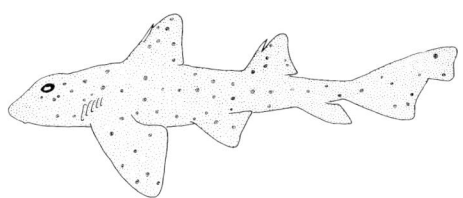

BULLHEAD SHARKS P. 17

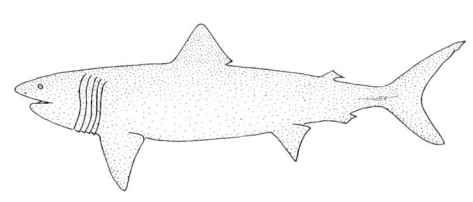

BASKING SHARKS P. 18

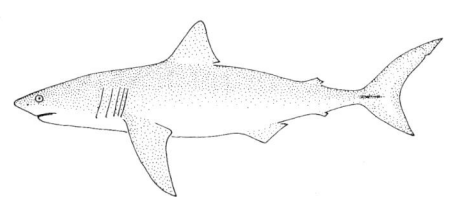

MACKEREL SHARKS P. 18

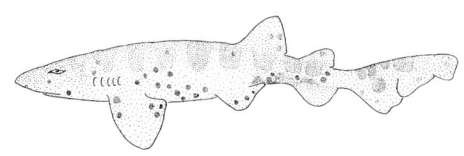

CAT SHARKS P. 19

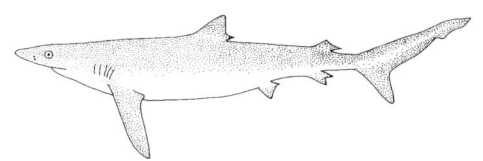

REQUIEM SHARKS P. 20

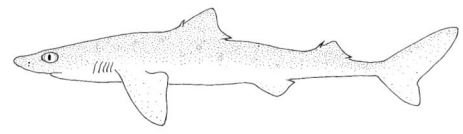

DOGFISH SHARKS P. 21

PICTORIAL KEY TO FISH FAMILIES

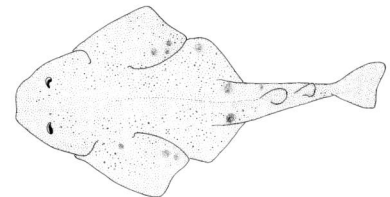

ANGEL SHARKS P. 22

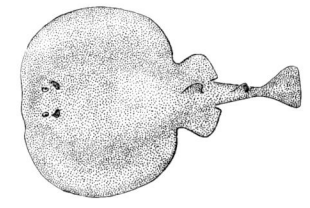

ELECTRIC RAYS P. 22

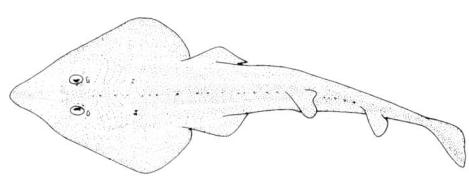

GUITARFISHES P. 23

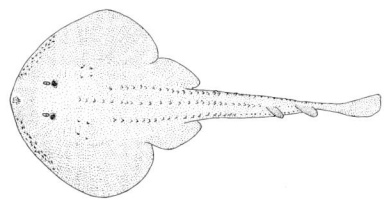

THORNBACK P. 24

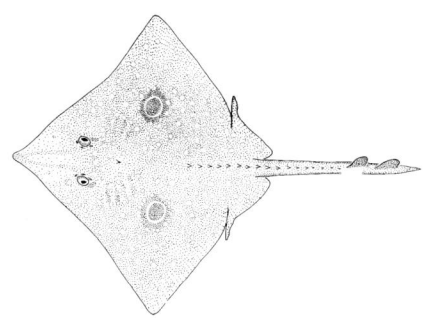

SKATES P. 24

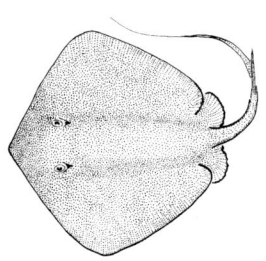

STINGRAYS P. 25

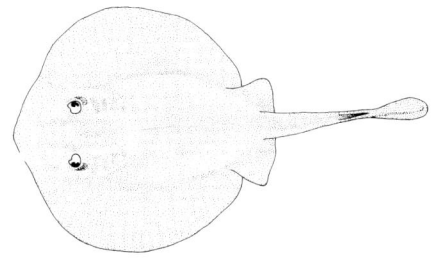

ROUND STINGRAYS P. 26

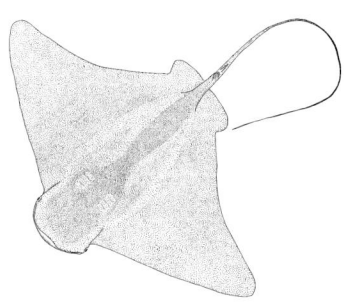

EAGLE RAYS P. 27

PICTORIAL KEY TO FISH FAMILIES

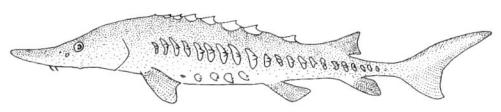

STURGEONS P. 27

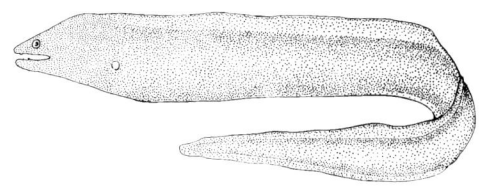

MORAYS P. 28

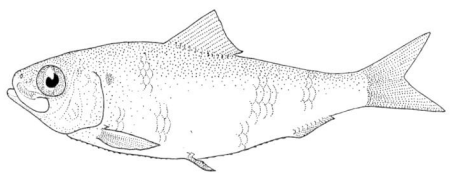

HERRINGS P. 29

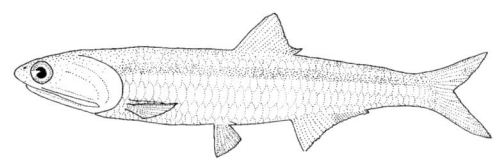

ANCHOVIES P. 30

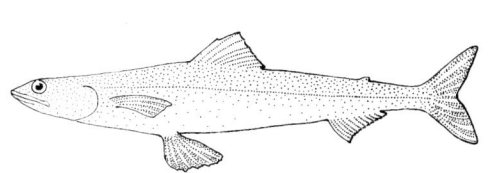

LIZARDFISHES P. 30

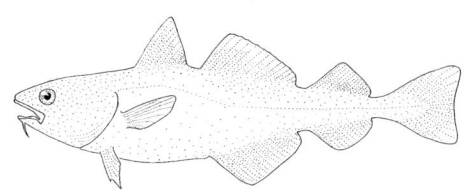

CODS P. 31

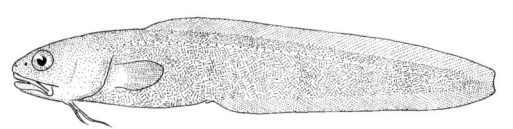

CUSK-EELS P. 32

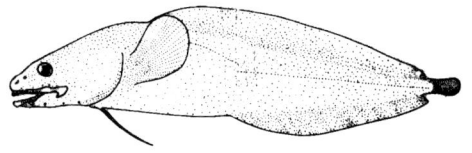

LIVEBEARING BROTULAS P. 33

PICTORIAL KEY TO FISH FAMILIES

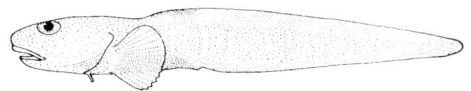

EELPOUTS P. 34

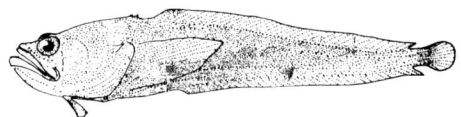

TOADFISHES P. 35

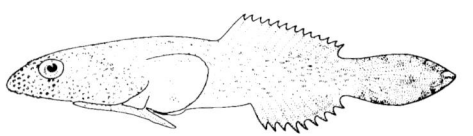

CLINGFISHES P. 35

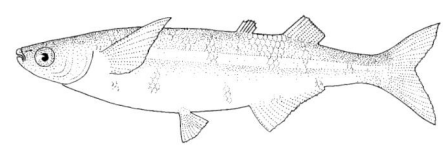

SILVERSIDES P. 36

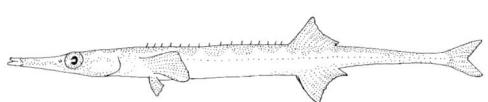

STICKLEBACKS P. 37

PIPEFISHES & SEAHORSES P. 38

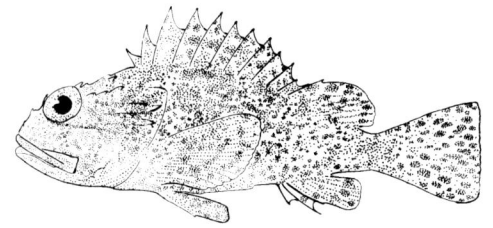

SCORPIONFISHES P. 39

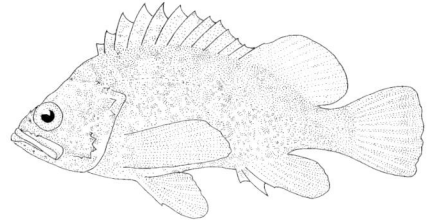

ROCKFISHES P. 39

PICTORIAL KEY TO FISH FAMILIES

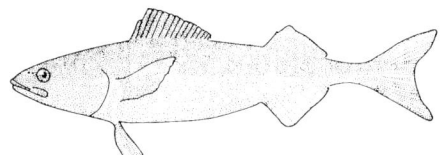

SABLEFISHES P. 53

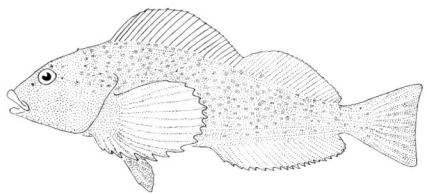

GREENLINGS & LINGCOD P. 53

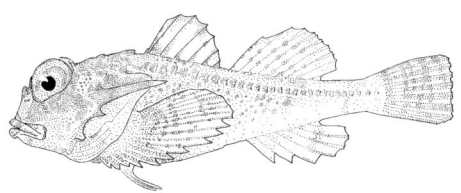

SCULPINS P. 56

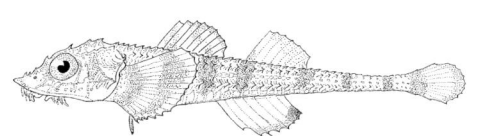

POACHERS P. 64

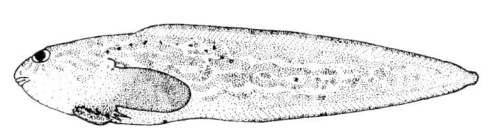

SNAIL FISHES P. 67

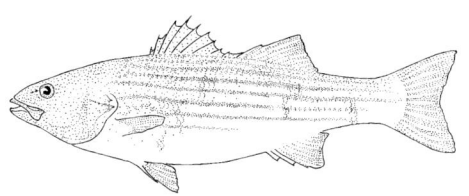

TEMPERATE BASSES P. 69

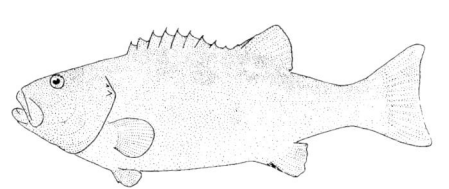

GIANT SEA BASSES P. 69

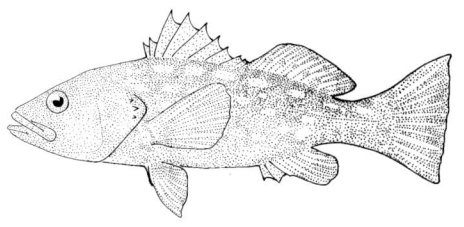

GROUPERS P. 70

PICTORIAL KEY TO FISH FAMILIES

BIG EYES P. 72

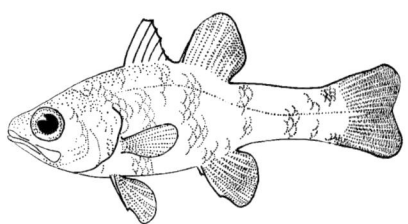

CARDINALFISHES P. 72

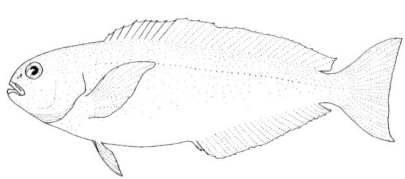

TILEFISHES P. 73

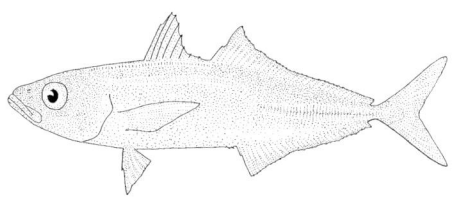

JACKS P. 74

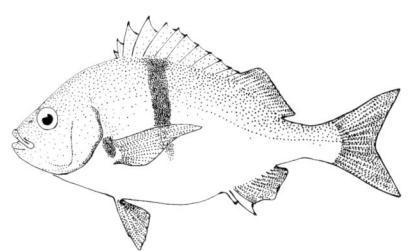

GRUNTS P. 75

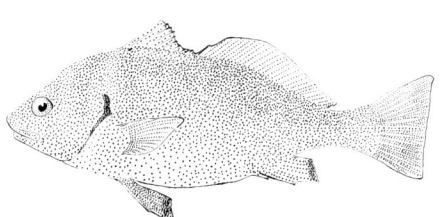

CROAKERS P. 76

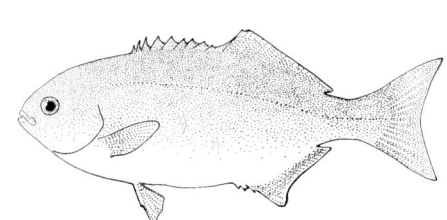

SEA CHUBS P. 77

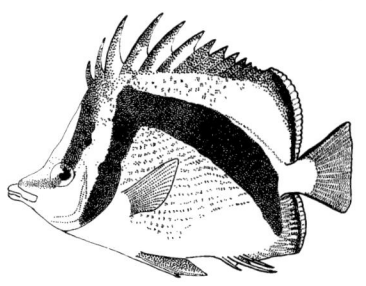

BUTTERFLYFISHES P. 79

PICTORIAL KEY TO FISH FAMILIES

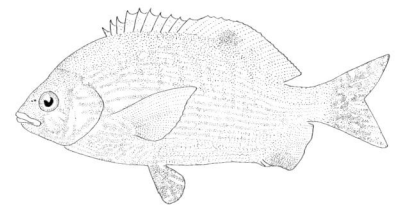

SURFPERCHES P. 80

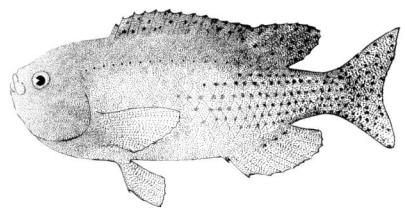

DAMSELFISHES P. 84

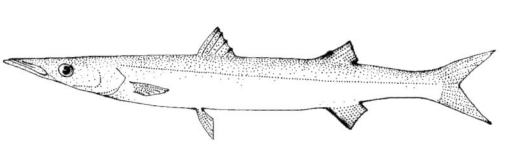

BARRACUDAS P. 86

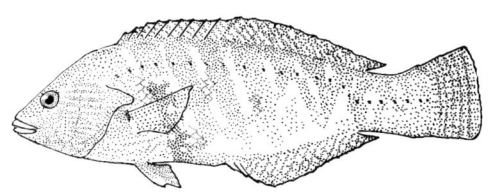

WRASSES P. 87

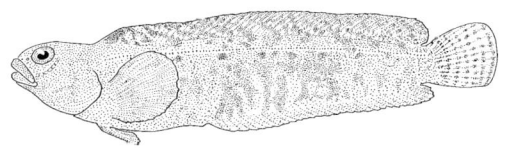

RONQUILS P. 90

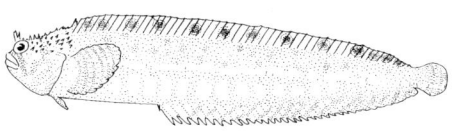

PRICKLEBACKS P. 92

WRYMOUTHS P. 94

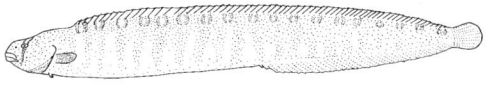

GUNNELS P. 95

PICTORIAL KEY TO FISH FAMILIES

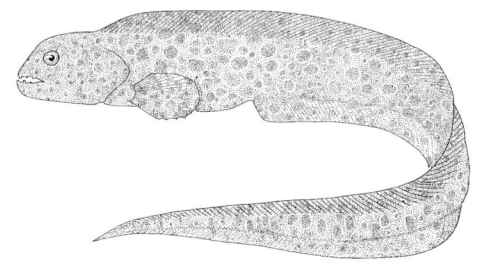

WOLFFISHES P. 97

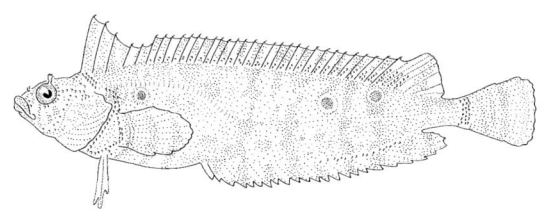

KELPFISHES & FRINGEHEADS P.97

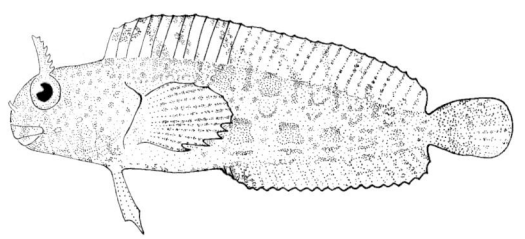

COMBTOOTH BLENNIES P. 100

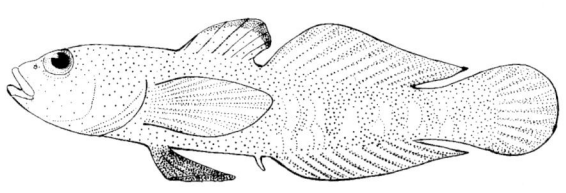

GOBIES P. 101

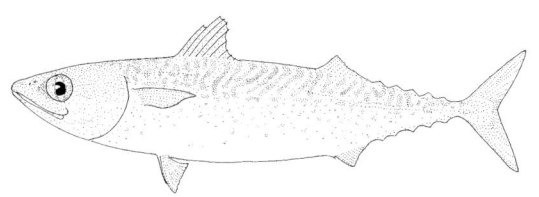

MACKERELS & TUNAS P. 103

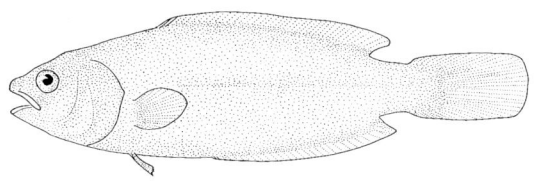

BUTTERFISHES P. 104

PICTORIAL KEY TO FISH FAMILIES

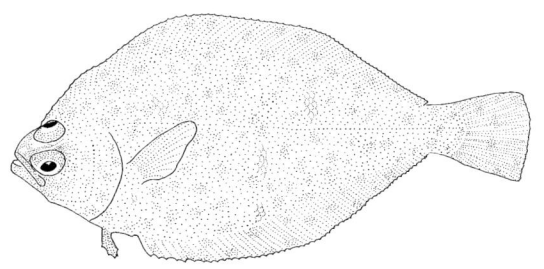

LEFTEYE FLOUNDERS P. 105

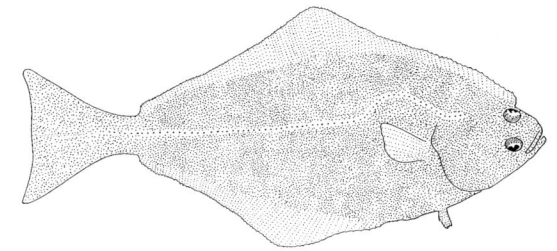

RIGHTEYE FLOUNDERS P. 106

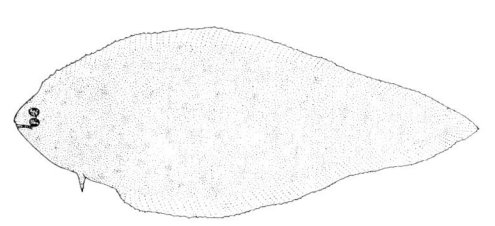

TONGUEFISHES P. 111

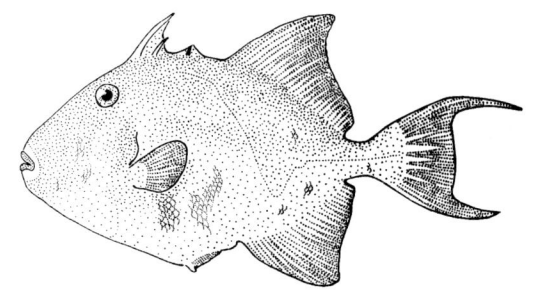

TRIGGERFISHES P. 112

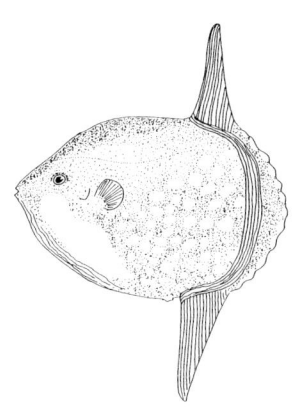

MOLAS P. 112

CLASS CHONDRICHTHYES
Cartilaginous Fishes

FAMILY CHIMAERIDAE
Chimaeras

The members of this ancient family of cartilaginous fishes have only one gill opening. There are two dorsal fins. A spine is present on the first of the two dorsal fins. Most members of the family lack denticles. The males possess a spiny clasping organ on the forehead, in addition to the claspers at each pelvic fin. Chimaeras, or ratfish, are found worldwide, usually in very deep water. There are about 35 species that have been described, three along our coast.

1. **SPOTTED RATFISH**   *Hydrolagus colliei*
Identification: This close relative to sharks and rays can easily be recognized by its smooth skin, long tapering tail, and bulky snout. *Size:* Length to 3.2 ft (1.0 m). *Range and Habitat:* Southeastern Alaska to Sebastian Vizcaino Bay, Baja California, with an isolated population in the upper Gulf of California. Found on soft bottoms, from shallow depths to 2995 ft (913 m). *Natural History:* Eggs are laid in elongated, ridged, brown cases. Spotted ratfish feed on clams, crustaceans and fishes. The venomous dorsal spine can inflict a painful wound, but is not fatal.

FAMILY HEXANCHIDAE
Cow Sharks

These primitive sharks have only one dorsal fin and live and feed near the bottom, usually in deep water, although some enter large bays. Cow sharks' eggs develop and hatch within the females (ovoviviparous).

Of the four known species only two occur along our coast, the sixgill shark, *Hexanchus griseus* and sevengill shark, *Notorynchus cepedianus.*

2. SIXGILL SHARK   *Hexanchus griseus*

Identification: The sixgill shark is the only shark in this region with six gill slits. The seven gill shark (*Notorynchus cepedianus,* not illustrated) is similar in appearance to the six gill shark, but these aggressive sharks have seven gill slits and black spots on the body. *Size: H. griseus:* Length to 9 ft (2.76 m), weight to 326 lbs. (148 kg). *N. cepedianus:* Length to 15.5 ft (4.7 m), weight 1300 lb (590 kg). *Range and Habitat: H. griseus:* Worldwide in temperate waters; on this coast, Aleutian Islands to northern California. *N. cepedianus:* Occurs in Atlantic, Pacific, and Indian oceans, on this coast from British Columbia to Gulf of California. Both species prefer soft bottoms, in deep bay channels and offshore waters. Sixgill shark adults have been captured from depths of 300 ft (91 m).

FAMILY HETERODONTIDAE
Bullhead Sharks

Bullhead sharks or horn sharks have a spine in front of each dorsal fin. These bottom dwellers are found in coastal waters and deposit hard grenade-shaped egg cases (oviparous) containing a single embryo. Eight species are known, but only one species occurs in our area.

3. HORN SHARK   *Heterodontus francisci*

Identification: A brown or gray colored shark with large black spots on body and spines in front of each dorsal fin. *Size:* Length to 4 ft (1.2 m. *Range and Habitat:* Monterey, California, to the Gulf of California, but not recorded from southern part of Gulf. Common around shallow rocky reefs in southern California. Maximum reported depth is 500 ft (153 m). *Natural History:* Horn sharks feed at night on crabs, shellfishes and sea urchins. Spawning takes place in the spring. It takes about 7 to 9 months for the eggs to hatch.

FAMILY CETORHINIDAE
Basking Sharks

The members of this family have big mouths, very large gill slits and long gill rakers, used for filtering out small planktonic prey. Basking sharks bear live young.

4. BASKING SHARK *Cetorhinus maximus*
Identification: The long gill slits that nearly meet under the throat are very distinctive. *Size:* Length to 45 ft (l3.7 m); weight to 8600 lbs. (3900 kg). *Range and Habitat:* Worldwide; on this coast from Aleutian Islands to Gulf of California. Found in pelagic and inshore areas; may migrate to deeper waters seasonally. *Natural History:* On the Pacific Coast, populations of these large sharks have apparently declined. Large schools that appeared regularly off southern and central California are now rarely observed. Basking sharks are plankton feeders and are usually observed on the surface when feeding.

FAMILY LAMNIDAE
Mackerel Sharks

Members of this family, including the notorious white shark, *Carcharodon carcharias,* are found in all the world's oceans. They are all viviparous and the young may obtain additional nourishment before birth by feeding on the eggs of their embryonic siblings. All members of the family are fast swimmers, preying on fish, mammals, turtles, birds and large squid. Three of the five known species occur off the Pacific Coast.

5. WHITE SHARK *Carcharodon carcharias*

Identification: This large, deep-bodied shark has a very large caudal keel. The first dorsal fin begins over the rear edge of the pectoral fin. The large teeth of this predator are triangular and have serrated edges. *Size:* Length to at least 21 ft (6.4 m). *Range and Habitat:* White sharks are found worldwide in near-shore temperate and tropical oceans, on this coast from the Gulf of Alaska to the Gulf of California, and in Chile. Most commonly found around seal rookeries from the surface to depths of about 4200 ft (1280 m). *Natural History:* This is the most dangerous shark in our waters. Adults feed on marine mammals, while juveniles subsist mostly on fish.

S. Drogin
D. Blodgett

6. SHORTFIN MAKO *Isurus oxyrinchus*

Identification: The heavy, streamlined body, long, conical, pointed snout; long pectoral fin, and crescent-shaped tail fin are good identification characters. *Size*: Length to 12.5 feet (3.8 m) and weight to 1102 lbs (500 kg). *Range and Habitat:* Worldwide in warm waters, on this coast from Oregon to the Gulf of California. Pelagic. *Natural History:* Believed to be the fastest swimming shark, the mako feeds on sardines, mackerels and other schooling fishes, as well as swordfish, blue sharks and squids. They have been implicated in attacks on humans.

FAMILY SCYLIORHINIDAE
Cat Sharks

Cat sharks have two dorsal fins that are located on the rear of the body. The first dorsal fin originates over or behind the origin of the pelvic fins. The eyes are long, slit-shaped, and are placed near the top of the flattened head. The tail fin is positioned horizontally rather than with vertical lobes. Most of these bottom dwelling sharks occur in very deep water in cold as well as warm seas. Many cat sharks lay eggs, but a few are ovoviviparous. They feed on fishes, crustaceans, cephalopods, clams, and echinoderms. Eighty-five species have been described, but only four occur in this area, three of which are found only in deep water.

7. SWELL SHARK
Cephaloscyllium ventriosum

Identification: The only spotted and mottled shallow water shark in our area with the first dorsal fin located behind origin of pelvic fins. *Size:* Length to 3.3 ft (1.0 m); weight to 60 lbs (27 k). *Range and Habitat:* Monterey Bay, California, to Acapulco, Mexico, and Chile; around shallow reefs in caves and crevices; in depths from shallow water to 1,380 ft (421 m). *Natural History:* This cryptic, sedentary shark lays individual eggs in distinctive amber-colored cases.

FAMILY CARCHARHINIDAE
Requiem Sharks

Requiem sharks have round or vertically oval eyes. A nictitating membrane is present. Most of the family occur in tropical seas nearshore as well as offshore. Most members of the family bear live young, the embryos receive nourishment from the mother (viviparous), but some develop and hatch from eggs retained by the female. They feed on a variety of fishes, invertebrates, marine mammals and sea turtles. There are approximately 75 known species. Nine species occur off our coast.

8. LEOPARD SHARK   *Triakis semifasciata*

Identification: The large black bars and spots on the body separate this shark from all other requiem sharks. *Size:* Length to 7 ft (2.1 m). *Range and Habitat:* Oregon to the Gulf of California; on sand and mud in bays and shallow inshore waters to depths of 300 ft (90 m). *Natural History:* Leopard sharks feed on fishes and invertebrates. They regularly are found in aggregations on or near the bottom in shallow inshore waters and bays during the summer. They bear live young; the 4 to 29 embryos develop within the female.

20

9. BLUE SHARK   *Prionace glauca*

Identification: This common surface (epipelagic) shark can be readily identified by the striking blue color above and gray-white below and the long saber-like pectoral fin. *Size:* Length to 13 ft (3.9 m). *Range and Habitat:* Worldwide; in eastern Pacific from the Gulf of Alaska to Chile. Common in our coastal surface water during late summer. *Natural History:* Up to 60 young sharks develop within the female. The adults feed on salmon, lanternfishes, squid, and other small fish.

M. Chamberlain

FAMILY SQUALIDAE
Dogfish Sharks

These mostly small sharks lack an anal fin. Most members of the family are found in deep water. The eggs develop within the female, and the young are born after a gestation of 22 to 26 months. This family contains about 70 species worldwide, but only 4 species occur off our coast.

10. SPINY DOGFISH   *Squalus acanthias*

Identification: This common shark also has spines in front of each dorsal fin, but it lacks the bull-shaped head and black spots of the horn shark. *Size:* Length to 5.2 ft (1.6 m). *Range and Habitat:* Temperate and subtropical Atlantic and Pacific Oceans; on our coast from Alaska to central Baja California. Over sand and mud bottoms. Occasionally seen near reefs in British Columbia. The maximum recorded depth is 2,400 ft (732 m). *Natural History:* These strong swimmers feed throughout the water column. It takes 13 and 23 years respectively for males and females to reach sexual maturity.

FAMILY SQUATINIDAE
Angel Sharks

The mouths of the members of these ray-shaped sharks are at the front of the flattened body. The very large pectoral fins have a free triangular lobe. Two dorsal fins are located near the tail. They lack an anal fin. All angel sharks are ovoviviparous and occur worldwide in shallow waters. There are approximately 12 species, but only one species occurs off our coast.

11. PACIFIC ANGEL SHARK
Squatina californica

Identification: The skate-like body is usually covered with brown spots; the gill slits are located in a notch on sides behind head. *Size:* Length to 5 ft (1.5 m); weight to 60 lbs (27 k). *Range and Habitat:* Southeastern Alaska to the Gulf of California, but not recorded from British Columbia. Common around southern California Channel Islands; on sand and mud in shallow water, often near reefs. *Natural History:* These ambush predators bury themselves in the sand or mud and wait for their small fish prey. Their numbers have been reduced substantially in recent years due to the commercial fishery.

FAMILY TORPEDINIDAE
Electric Rays

Electric rays have oval bodies (discs) and large, symmetrical tail fins. The wide mouth is ideal for capturing fishes that have been stunned by the powerful electric charge. About 14 species worldwide. Only one species is found in this region.

12. PACIFIC ELECTRIC RAY
Torpedo californica

Identification: The only ray in our area that lacks spines or prickles. The large caudal fin and spots on the dorsal surface are also distinctive. *Size:* Length to 4.5 ft (1.4 m); weight to 90 lbs. (41 kg). *Range and Habitat:* Queen Charlotte Islands, British Columbia, to Sebastian Vizcaino Bay, Baja California. On mud and sand bottoms; to depths of 1,380 ft (421 m). *Natural History:* These rays lack a venomous spine but are capable of producing a strong electrical shock of up to 80 volts. They are aggressive and divers have reported unprovoked attacks. Young develop within female.

FAMILY RHINOBATIDAE
Guitarfishes

These rays have a narrower head (disc) than other rays. They have two dorsal fins located on the thick posterior body. There are usually one or more rows of spines on the back and the body is covered with denticles. Almost all bear live young (ovoviviparous), but some species may lay eggs. There are about 43 species worldwide. Three have been recorded off the Pacific Coast of North America.

13. SHOVELNOSE GUITARFISH
Rhinobatis productus

Identification: This species has a long pointed snout, and there is only one row of spines along the back. They lack any distinctive markings on the sandy-brown upper body. *Size:* Length to 5.5 ft (1.7 m), weight to 40.5 lbs (18.4 kg). *Range and Habitat:* These bottom dwellers have been recorded from San Francisco, California, to the Gulf of California on sand or sand/mud substrate in shallow depths to about 60 feet (18 m). *Natural History:* These rays feed on a variety of crabs, worms, clams and fishes. A female may give birth to as many as 28 juveniles, which are about 6 inches (15 cm) in length.

14. BANDED GUITARFISH
Zapteryx exasperata

Identification: The banded guitarfish differs from the shovelnose guitarfish by having a disc about as wide as long in adults and many dark bands across the back. *Size:* Length to 3 ft (90 cm); *Range and Habitat:* Newport Beach, California, to Panama.

15. THORNBACK *Platyrhinoidis triseriata*

Identification: The three rows of prominent spines on the dorsal surface of adults, and the rounded disc separate this species from the other guitarfishes in our area. *Size:* Length to 3 ft (90 cm). *Range and Habitat:* Tomales Bay, California, to Thurloe Head, Baja California Sur; on sand and mud bottoms; to depths of 150 ft (46 m). *Natural History:* Thornbacks feed on crustaceans, worms and molluscs. They are ovoviviparous.

FAMILY RAJIDAE
Skates

This family contains more species than any other of the sharks and rays. The body and tail are covered with denticles and spines. Most members have two dorsal fins located near the small caudal fin. Skates are found in all temperate seas in shallow to deep waters. In the tropics they occur only in deep waters, to at least 9000 feet (2600 m). There are 177 known species, and at least 11 species have been reported in this region.

16. BIG SKATE   *Raja binoculata*

Identification: The big skate is the only member of the family in our area commonly encountered by divers. It can be distinguished by the two large eye spots (ocelli), one on each wing, and the shallow notch on the rear edge of the pelvic fins. *Size:* Length to 8 ft (2.4 m), weight to 200 pounds (91 kg). *Range and Habitat:* Bering Sea to Cedros Island, Baja California; on sand and mud in depths from 10 to 360 ft (3 to 110 m). *Natural History:* Skates lay their eggs in individual horny cases. Big skates feed on crustaceans and fishes.

FAMILY DASYATIDAE
Stingrays

Stingrays lack dorsal fins and, usually, a caudal fin. There are one or two venomous spines on the tail. They bear live young (ovoviviparous). About 100 species have been observed worldwide. Only three species occur off this coast north of Baja California.

M. Chamberlain

17. PELAGIC STINGRAY *Dasyatis violacea*

Description: The diamond shaped disc is rounded in front. The tail is very long, at least twice the length of the body and has a very long venomous spine. *Size:* Length to 5.3 feet (163 cm). *Range and Habitat:* As their common name indicates, these rays live offshore in warm, near-surface waters, in most of the world's oceans; on this coast from British Columbia to the Galapagos Islands. *Natural History:* Blue-water divers visiting offshore kelp paddies occasionally see these interesting rays. They feed on shrimps, squids and fishes.

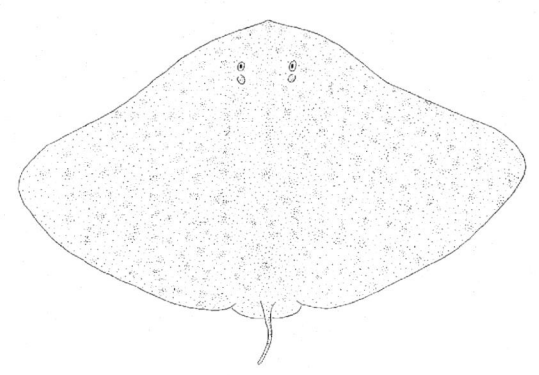

18. CALIFORNIA BUTTERFLY RAY
Gymnura marmorata

Identification: California butterfly rays have very short tails and wide discs that are about twice as wide as long. *Size:* Width to 5 ft (1.5 m). *Range and Habitat:* Point Conception, California, to Peru. Common in shallow bays and off sandy beaches in southern California. *Natural History:* Butterfly rays feed on a variety of clams, crustaceans and fishes. When not feeding they spend most of their time buried in the sand or mud.

FAMILY UROLOPHIDAE
Round Stingrays

These stingrays differ from the previous family members by having a distinct caudal fin and short and broad tails. Round stingrays are found in all the world's tropical and semi- tropical seas. They bear live young and the developing embryos receive nourishment from the lining of the uterus. There are 34 species known worldwide; on this coast only one species occurs north of Baja California.

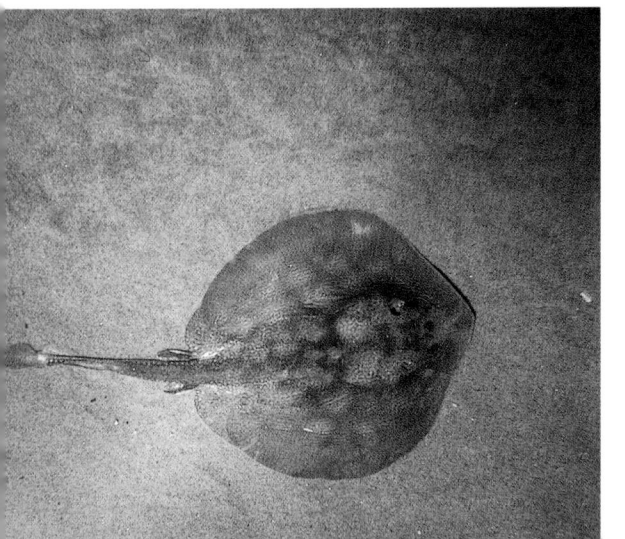

19. ROUND STINGRAY   *Urolophus halleri*

Identification: The almost circular disc, sometimes mottled or with spots or other markings, is distinctive. *Size:* Length to 22 inches (56 cm). *Range and Habitat:* Humboldt Bay, California, to Panama. On sand and mud bottoms, occasionally on reefs in depths to 70 ft (21 m). *Natural History:* Feed on shrimps, crabs, snails, and clams.

26

FAMILY MYLIOBATIDAE
Eagle Rays

Eagle rays have large heads that are elevated above the disc. The long slender tails have no caudal fin. There is a large dorsal fin at the base of the tail and the sting is located close behind. These rays have large jaws with platelike teeth that are used to crush their prey of clams, oysters and scallops. Eagle rays occur worldwide in warm as well as temperate waters. They are ovoviviparous. About 20 species have been described, but only one occurs in our area.

20. BAT RAY   *Myliobatis californica*
Identification: The only stingray in our area with a large head that protrudes beyond the anterior edge of the disc. *Size:* Width to 6 ft (1.8 m); weight to 210 lbs (95 kg). *Range and Habitat:* Oregon to the Gulf of California. In bays and other shallow, sandy, or mud bottoms; to depths of 150 ft (45 m). *Natural History:* Bat rays feed on clams, oysters, abalone and crabs. Mating takes place during the summer. Litters usually do not exceed 10.

CLASS OSTEICHTHYES
Bony Fishes

FAMILY ACIPENSERIDAE
Sturgeons

Sturgeons are ancient bottom dwellers that have five rows of scutes (bony plates) along the body. The scutes almost disappear in old adults. The bony head is distinctive with the long snout and the barbels in front of the mouth. Adults lack teeth. There is only one dorsal fin, and the caudal fin possesses a much longer upper lobe than the lower lobe. Family members occur in North America, Europe and Asia. All members spawn in freshwater, and some spend the rest of their time in salt or brackish seas, particularly in bays and estuaries. There are about 25 recorded species, but only two on this coast.

21. GREEN STURGEON
Acipenser medirostris

Identification: Both sturgeon species are occasionally observed by divers in this area. The green sturgeon is identifiable by 23 to 30 bony scutes on each side and 1 to 2 scutes behind the dorsal fin. The white sturgeon (*Acipenser transmontanus,* not illustrated) has 38 to 48 bony scutes on each side and no scutes behind the dorsal fin. *Size: A medirostris:* Length to 7 ft (2.1 m); weight to 350 lbs. (159 kg). *A. transmontanus:* Length to 20 ft (6 m); weight to 1800 lb (816 kg). *Range and Habitat: A. medirostris:* Japan to Bering Sea and south to Ensenada, Baja California. *A. transmontanus:* Alaska to Ensenada, Baja California. Both species on soft bottoms to depths of 400 ft (122 m).

FAMILY MURAENIDAE
Morays

Morays lack pectoral fins, usually have well developed canine teeth, and the gill openings are round and very reduced. They also lack scales and a lateral line. The members of this family are common in shallow tropical seas amongst coral or rocky reefs; some species occur at depths of 1600 ft. (489 m). About 200 species have been described. There is only one species that has been recorded north of central Baja California.

22. CALIFORNIA MORAY
Gymnothorax mordax

Identification: This is the only member of the family in our area and can be distinguished from other eel-like fishes by the lack of pectoral and pelvic fins. *Size:* Length to 5 ft (1.5 m). *Range and Habitat:* Point Conception, California, to Magdalena Bay, Baja California Sur. In rocky caves and crevices; from shallow water to about 130 ft (40 m). *Natural History:* Morays feed on crabs, fish, lobster, and sea urchins. The rarely encountered larvae (leptocephali) occur in offshore surface waters.

FAMILY CLUPEIDAE
Herrings

The members of this very important family provide food for a host of game and commercially important fishes, as well as being sought out by commercial fisheries worldwide. Most have compressed bodies. All lack an adipose fin and, except one, a lateral line. The pelvic fins are located closer to the anus than to the gill opening. Herrings are schooling fishes that occur in all tropical and temperate oceans, in bays and near shore waters; a few species occur in freshwater. There are about 200 species worldwide; 6 are recorded from this area.

23. PACIFIC HERRING *Clupea pallasii*
Identification: The silvery body lacks black spots on the sides. The pelvic fins are located under the dorsal fin. The last dorsal fin ray is no longer than the other rays, and there are no striations on the gill cover. *Size:* Length to l8 inches (46 cm). *Range and Habitat:* Korea and Japan north to Arctic Alaska and south to northern Baja California. Schools of these fish frequent bays during spawning, offshore and inshore waters rest of year. *Natural History:* Spawning takes place during winter months. A female can lay up to l25,000 eggs, which are attached to kelp, eel grass and other objects.

24. PACIFIC SARDINE *Sardinops sagax*
Identification: Pacific sardines have scales or scutes, on the midline between the pelvic fins and anal fin with fine points that protrude beyond rear edge of the scale. Pacific sardines also have a row of black spots just above the lateral line on each side; the gill cover has striations. *Size:* Length to 16.3 inches (4l cm). *Range and Habitat:* Kamchatka to southeastern Alaska and south to Guaymas, Mexico. *Natural History:* Sardines are pelagic, occurring in large schools near shore. They sometimes mix with other pelagic species such as jack mackerel or Pacific mackerel.

FAMILY ENGRAULIDIDAE
Anchovies

These small silvery fishes have long snouts that overhang the mouth. Anchovies also have a very long upper jaw that extends past the eye. Family members lack fin spines, an adipose fin, and a lateral line. Anchovies occur in large schools in all the world's warmer oceans. Most are found near shore; a few species occur in freshwater. They are very important prey for a host of predatory fishes, birds and mammals. They are also important commercially for bait, food and oil. There are about 140 species worldwide; 4 species have been reported from this area.

25. NORTHERN ANCHOVY
Engraulis mordax

Identification: Northern anchovies have an auxiliary scale adjacent to each pectoral fin. The mouth is very large, with upper jaw bone (maxillary) reaching the rear edge of the gill cover. *Size:* Length to at least 9 inches (23 cm). *Range and Habitat:* Queen Charlotte Islands, British Columbia, to Cabo San Lucas, Baja California Sur, and the Gulf of California. *Natural History:* The northern anchovy is the most abundant anchovy on this coast. Anchovies are pelagic, occurring in large, tightly packed schools.

FAMILY SYNODONTIDAE
Lizardfishes

Lizardfishes have rounded bodies when viewed in cross section and large tooth-filled mouths. The single dorsal fin is located at about mid body. Members of this family have adipose fins (except for the adult of an Australian species). The origin of the pelvic fins is located in front of the origin of the dorsal fin. These tropical fishes are found in tropical seas worldwide, usually on soft bottoms, but also on reefs. Worldwide about 35 species are recognized, but only one species occurs in our area.

26. CALIFORNIA LIZARDFISH
Synodus lucioceps

Identification: The body shape, broad triangular-shaped head, and adipose fin instead of a rayed second dorsal are good distinguishing characters. *Size:* Length to 25.2 inches (64 cm). *Range and Habitat:* San Francisco, California, to Guaymas, Sonora, Mexico. On sand and mud; from 5 to 750 ft deep (2 to 229 m). *Natural History:* Lizardfish feed on other fish and squid.

FAMILY GADIDAE
Cods

Cods are elongate fishes covered with small cycloid scales. The pelvic fins are located slightly in front of the pectoral fins (thoracic). Many species have three dorsal fins, two anal fins and square-cut caudal fins. The members of this family inhabit cool seas worldwide; two species have been recorded in freshwater. Only three species are known from the coast, but 75 species are recognized worldwide.

N. McDaniel

27. PACIFIC COD   *Gadus macrocephalus*
Identification: The Pacific cod has three dorsal fins, two anal fins and a barbel as long as or longer than the diameter of the eye. *Size:* Length to 45 inches (114 cm). *Range and Habitat:* Japan to Bering Sea to Santa Monica Bay, California. Over deep reefs and soft bottoms; from 40 to 1800 ft (12 to 549 m). *Natural History:* A very important commercial fish off British Columbia and Alaska. Large females can produce over a million eggs.

28. PACIFIC TOMCOD
Microgadus proximus

Identification: Can be distinguished from the Pacific cod by the lower jaw, which is shorter than the upper, and a barbel shorter than eye diameter. *Size:* Length to 12 inches (30 cm). *Range and Habitat:* Bering Sea to Point Sal, California. A midwater and bottom dweller; to depths of 90 to 720 ft (27 to 219 m). The young are found in shallow waters, often near the surface. *Natural History:* Pacific tomcod provide food for a number of other fishes.

G. Jensen
L. Barr

29. WALLEYE POLLOCK
Theragra chalcogramma

Identification: Distinguished from other cods by the slightly projecting lower jaw and the lack of a barbel. *Size:* Length to 3 ft (91 cm). *Range and Habitat:* Japan and Bering Sea, to Carmel Bay, California. Over reefs and soft bottoms; found near the surface to 1200 ft (366 m). *Natural History:* Walleye pollock feed on shrimp, herring, young salmon, and other fish. They in turn are fed on by seals, sea lions, porpoises and other fishes.

FAMILY OPHIDIIDAE
Cusk-Eels

The "letter opener"-like tapered body and very long dorsal and anal fins that reach or connect to the pointed caudal fin are characters of this family. The pelvic fins, when present, are located under or in front of the gill openings. Cusk-eels are found in tropical as well as temperate waters; a few occur in fresh water. Some, that live in caves, or in the deep sea, are blind. Of the 190 species known, five occur off our coast, but only two species occur in shallow waters.

30. **SPOTTED CUSK-EEL**   *Chilara taylori*

Identification: Distinguished by the eel-like body and pelvic fins near tip of lower jaw. The spotted cusk-eel differs from the more southern basketweave cusk-eel, *Ophidion scrippsae* (not illustrated), by having dark spotting on the back and sides. *Size: Chilara taylori:* Length to 14.3 inches (36 cm); *Ophidion scrippsae:* to 10.8 inches (27 cm). *Range and Habitat: C. taylori:* Oregon to Magdalena Bay, Baja California Sur; *O. scrippsae:* Pt. Arguello, California, to Magdalena Bay, Baja California Sur. On sand and mud bottoms; to depths of 4 to 800 ft (1.2 - 244m) and 9 to 230 ft (2.7 - 70 m). *Natural History:* Cusk-eels burrow tail first into the sand or mud. Young spotted cusk-eels, under 4 inches, lack spots. Rarely seen during daylight, they are commonly observed out of their borrows at night. These small fish provide food for sea lions and cormorants.

FAMILY BYTHITIDAE
Livebearing Brotulas

Brotulas have body shapes similar to the cusk-eels; however, the pelvic fins when present are located under the gill openings. Males possess a copulatory organ. Some species have scales. Members of this family occur in fresh water as well as in the ocean; some species are known only from the very deep seas. About l50 species have been described worldwide. There are two shallow water and one deep water brotulids in this area.

31. **RED BROTULA**
       Brosmophycis marginata

Identification: These nocturnal crevice dwellers have dark red-brown bodies with red fins. The caudal fin is separated from the long dorsal and anal fins. The very slender (only two rays) pelvic fins are located beneath the gill openings. *Size:* Length to 18 inches (46 cm). *Range and Habitat:* Petersburg, Alaska, to Ensenada Bay, Baja California, in rocky areas to depths of 10 to 84 ft (3-25.6 m). *Natural History:* Brotulas bear live young.

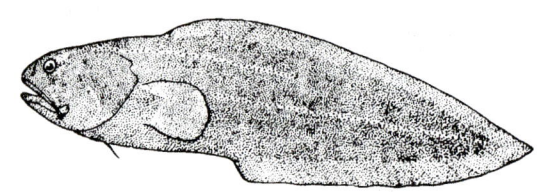

32. PURPLE BROTULA
Oligopus diagrammus

Identification: This rarely observed gray to purplish black brotula has dorsal and anal fins joined to the caudal fin. The pelvic fin has only one ray and there are two lateral lines. *Size:* Length to 8 inches (20 cm). *Range and Habitat:* San Clemente Island, California, to Panama and the Galapagos Islands. These brotulas frequent rocky areas in caves and crevices. Depth range from l8 to 60 ft (5.5m - 18 m). *Natural History:* Like most members of the family this species is active only during darkness.

FAMILY ZOARCIDAE
Eelpouts

The dorsal and anal fins of these elongate fishes extend around the pointed tail. The members of this relatively large family have an upper jaw that extends beyond the lower jaw, often with large mouths and thick lips. Eelpouts either lack pelvic fins or if present are very small and located on the breast in advance of the pectoral fins. The members of this family are found worldwide in cold waters, including the Antarctic Ocean. These bottom dwellers occur in shallow areas, as well as in the very deep oceans; a few are members of the mid-water community. Of the 200+ known species 35 to 40 occur off our coast.

G. Jensen

33. BLACKBELLY EELPOUT
Lycodes pacificus

Identification: This species has small pelvic fins. The front of the dorsal fin, as well as the belly, is black. The rear portion of the dorsal and anal fins have black edges. *Size:* Length to 18 inches (46 cm). *Range and Habitat:* Gulf of Alaska to northern Baja California on soft bottoms. Depth ranges from 30 to l308 ft (9l to 399 m). *Natural History:* This eelpout provides food for sablefish (#76) and a variety of rockfishes. Large numbers are caught and discarded incidentally by commercial trawlers.

34

FAMILY BATRACHOIDIDAE
Toadfishes

Toadfishes have very large heads with respect to the tapering body. The small first dorsal fin has 2 to 4 spines and the long second dorsal fin is composed entirely of soft rays. The long anal fin also lacks spines. The pelvic fins are located ahead of the pectoral fins. There is a strong spine on the gill cover. Most members of the family lack scales. Toadfishes occur in shallow inshore waters of the world's tropical seas. A few of these bottom-dwellers occur in cold or temperate waters, and a few species live in freshwater. There are about 50 species recognized worldwide; only two species occur off our coast.

34. PLAINFIN MIDSHIPMAN
Porichthys notatus

Identification: The large head, scaleless body, and luminous organs (photophores) are very distinctive. The plainfin midshipman can be separated from the specklefin midshipman, *P. myriaster* (not illustrated), by the lack of spots on any of its fins. *Size: P. notatus:* Length to 15 inches (38 cm). *P. myriaster,* length to 20 inches (51 cm). *Range and Habitat: P. notatus,* Sitka, Alaska, to Gulf of California; *P. myriaster,* Pt. Conception, California, to Magdalena Bay, Baja California. On sand and mud bottoms; to depths of 1,000 ft (333 m) and 414 ft (126 m), respectively. *Natural History:* Spawning takes place in late spring and summer. The humming or grunting sound made by these fish occurs during the spawning season. The males guard the eggs that the females attach to the underside of rocks.

FAMILY GOBIESOCIDAE
Clingfishes

Clingfishes, as the name implies, have a sucking disc on their breast between the pectoral fins. The dorsal and anal fins are located far back on the body. There are no spines in the fins and no scales are present. This family is represented in tropical and temperate areas of all the world's oceans. A few species occur in freshwater. Of the 140 species known worldwide only 7 species occur in our area.

35. NORTHERN CLINGFISH
Gobiesox maeandricus

Identification: This clingfish can be separated from the six other species of clingfish that occur along this coast by its robust form, large head and suction disc. *Size:* Length to 6.5 inches (16 cm). *Range and Habitat:* Alaska to northern Baja California and the Revillagigedo Islands; intertidal areas, kelp beds, and around rocky subtidal areas to depths of at least 26 ft (7.9 m). *Natural History:* Clingfish are rarely observed in the open. They are usually found under rocks or in crevices.

F. Bavendam
R. Borema

36. KELP CLINGFISH *Rimicola muscarum*

Identification: This is the most common clingfish found in the kelp canopy, and the only slender clingfish found north of Monterey. The dorsal and anal fins are much shorter than those of the northern clingfish. *Size:* Length to 2.75 in (7 cm). *Range and Habitat:* Queen Charlotte Islands, British Columbia, to northern Baja California. Clings to kelp and eelgrass.

FAMILY ATHERINIDAE
Silversides

Silversides have two dorsal fins and lack a lateral line. They usually have small mouths and the pelvic fins are in the abdominal position. This family is represented worldwide in tropical and temperate oceans. Most species are found in marine environments, some in freshwater. Of the approximately 150 species, only three occur off our coast.

37. TOPSMELT — *Atherinops affinis*

Identification: Topsmelt can be distinguished from the larger jacksmelt, *Atherinopsis californiensis,* by the presence of five to eight scales on the back between the two dorsal fins and the forked teeth in one row. Jacksmelt have 10 to 12 scales between the dorsal fins and no forked teeth. *Size:* Length to 14.5 inches (37 cm). *Range and Habitat:* Sooke Harbour, Vancouver Island, British Columbia, to the Gulf of California; in bays, sloughs, and other shallow waters. *Natural History:* Topsmelt are surface dwellers and feeders that provide food for a number of fish eating predators, including man. They most commonly enter the catch of sport anglers fishing from piers.

38. JACKSMELT *Atherinopsis californiensis*

Identification: The anal fin of jacksmelt originates behind the first dorsal fin. There are 10 to 12 scales between the rear of the first dorsal fin and origin of the second dorsal fin. *Size:* Length to 17.5 inches (44 cm). *Range and Habitat:* Yakima, Oregon, to Santa Maria Bay, Baja California; near surface, inshore and in bays around piers, jetties, and kelp beds. *Natural History:* Jacksmelt are caught commercially for the fresh fish markets. They are also sought after by sport anglers and predatory fishes.

FAMILY GASTEROSTEIDAE
Sticklebacks

Members of this family have 2-26 isolated spines in front of the soft-rayed dorsal fin. Sticklebacks usually have bony plates on their sides instead normal of scales. These small fish occur in both fresh- as well as saltwater in the Northern Hemisphere. There are about 10 species, two of which occur off our coast.

39. TUBESNOUT   *Aulorhynchus flavidus*

Identification: The long snout and 23 to 26 isolated spines in front of the dorsal fin are distinctive. *Size:* Length to 7 inches (18 cm). *Range and Habitat:* Prince William Sound, Alaska, to Point Rompiente, Baja California Sur. In eel grass and kelp beds, from shallow bays to l00 ft (30 m). *Natural History:* Tubesnouts are nest builders; the nests are constructed and defended by the males.

40. THREESPINE STICKLEBACK
Gasterosteus aculeatus

Identification: The three isolated spines in front of the dorsal fin and the bony plates on the sides are distinctive. This stickleback also has keels on the caudal peduncle and one spine in the pelvic fin. *Size:* Length to 4 in (10 cm). *Range and Habitat:* From Korea and Bering Sea to northern Baja California. Usually found nearshore to depths of 90 feet (27 m) and in bays and estuaries as well as freshwater. *Natural History:* Threespine sticklebacks are anadromous. They spawn in freshwater where males build nests to attract females. The male guards the eggs. They feed on small crustaceans and fishes and are fed on by other fishes and birds.

FAMILY SYNGNATHIDAE
Pipefishes and Seahorses

The bodies of members of this family are enclosed in bony rings. These fishes have small, toothless mouths and long snouts. There is only one dorsal fin and no pelvic fins. Males have a broad pouch in which to carry eggs produced by the female. Pipefishes and seahorses occur worldwide in cold and warm seas. Most live in the ocean, but a few enter rivers. These shallow water dwellers are usually found around eelgrass and other marine plants, as well as sponges, gorgonians and corals. There are about 175 recognized species worldwide, but only seven on our coast.

41. PACIFIC SEAHORSE
Hippocampus ingens

Identification: The only seahorse on this coast; easily identified by the horse-shaped head and the absence of a caudal fin; the body is covered with bony rings. *Size:* Length to 1 ft (30 cm). *Range and Habitat:* San Clemente Island, California, to Peru, around shallow reefs, eel beds, and man-made structures. Pacific seahorses are most commonly found hanging on gorgonians and sponges. *Natural History:* This species is not common north of Baja California. The best place to observe them in California is in Mission Bay, San Diego, California.

42. BAY PIPEFISH
Syngnathus leptorhynchus

Identification: There are six species of pipefishes that occur in the area; two species are occasionally observed by divers and snorkelers, the bay pipefish and the kelp pipefish. All of the pipefishes are difficult to identify, even when you have them in hand. Bay pipefish, *Syngnathus leptorhynchus,* have 53 to 63 body rings and 28 to 43 dorsal fin rays; kelp pipefish, *S. californiensis,* have 46 to 52 body rings and 40 to 48 dorsal fin rays. *Size: S. leptorhynchus,* length to 13 inches (33 cm). *S. californiensis,* length to 19.5 inches (50 cm). *Range and Habitat: S. leptorhynchus:* Sitka, Alaska, to Guerrero Negro Lagoon, Baja California; in eelgrass in bays and sloughs. *S. californiensis:* Bodega Bay, California, to Santa Maria Bay, Baja Califonia; usually in kelp beds to depths of 48 ft (15 m).

FAMILY SCORPAENIDAE
Scorpionfishes and Rockfishes

There are more recognized species of scorpaenids (65 species) along our coast than of any other family. Scorpionfishes and rockfishes are recognized by a bone under the cheek (a suborbital stay) and most species have spines on their heads. The fin spines are mildly to strongly venomous, but the venom, in most species found in the area covered by this field guide, is weak. Fertilization of the eggs is internal. The scorpionfishes often deposit their eggs in gelatinous masses. The rockfishes are all ovoviparous; the eggs develop within the female and receive their nutrition from a yolk sac. Scorpionfishes are found in all warm seas, while rockfishes are limited to colder waters in the northern and southern hemispheres. On our coast there are three species of scorpionfishes and 62 species of rockfishes.

43. CALIFORNIA SCORPIONFISH
Scorpaena guttata

Identification: Distinguished from other members of the family by having only 8 to 10 dorsal rays, 12 spines in the dorsal fin. The pectoral fin is large and fan-shaped. *Size:* Length to 17 inches (43 cm). *Range and Habitat:* Santa Cruz, California, to Uncle Sam Bank, Baja California, and an isolated population in the Gulf of California; on rocky reefs to 600 ft (183 m). *Natural History:* Spotted scorpionfish lay eggs embedded in transparent, pear-shaped cases.

44. RAINBOW SCORPIONFISH
Scorpaenodes xyris

Identification: The large, dark spot on rear edge of the gill cover and 13 spines in the dorsal fin separate this small scorpionfish from the more common California scorpionfish. *Size:* Length to 6 inches (15 cm). *Range and Habitat:* Santa Catalina Island, California, to Peru, including the Gulf of California and other offshore islands; to depths of about 85 ft (26 m). *Natural History:* These scorpionfish live in caves and crevices and are rarely observed out in the open during daytime.

45. CHILIPEPPER *Sebastes goodei*

Identification: Chilipeppers are often confused with bocaccio (#46), but can be separated by the shorter maxillary, which does not extend beyond middle of eye. The chilipepper's anal fin is shorter and has only eight soft rays, compared to nine for bocaccio. Adults are reddish pink above and white below; young fish are light olive above. *Size:* Length to 22 inches (56 cm). *Range and Habitat:* Vancouver Island, British Columbia, to Magdalena Bay, Baja California Sur; around reefs as well as over soft bottoms. Adults found in deep water, 200 to 1080 ft (61 to 329 m). Juveniles (first year of life) occur in inshore waters as shallow as 50 ft (15 m). *Natural History:* Chilipeppers feed on krill, squid and fishes.

46. BOCACCIO   *Sebastes paucispinis*

Identification: The large mouth, with the maxillary extending to behind the eye, the dark back of the adult, and spots on the juvenile will help separate the bocaccio from its look-alike, the chilipepper, *S. goodei (#45). Size:* Length to 42 inches (107 cm). *Range and Habitat:* Stepovak Bay (Alaska Peninsula), Alaska, to Punta Blanca, Baja California; over rocky reefs and soft bottoms; from surface to 1580 ft (475 m). *Natural History:* As with all rockfish, the embryos develop into larvae within the female. Bocaccio feed mostly on other fishes. Bocaccio live at least 30 years. The population of this large, once commercially important rockfish is seriously depleted.

Juvenile
Adult

N. McDaniel

47. SILVERGRAY ROCKFISH
Sebastes brevispinus

Identification: Silvergray rockfish have large, upturned mouths with strongly projecting chins. The spines on the head are weak and usually only four pairs are present. *Size:* Length to 28 inches (71 cm). *Range and Habitat:* Bering Sea to Santa Barbara Island, California; around reefs and over soft bottoms to depths of 100 to 1200 ft (33 to 366 m). *Natural History:* These fish are rarely caught off California, but they are an important commercial species from Oregon to southeastern Alaska.

41

Juvenile

48. BLACK ROCKFISH   *Sebastes melanops*

Identification: Can be distinguished from the blue rockfish (#49) and the dusky rockfish (#50) by the larger maxillary, which extends to beneath the rear of the eye, and the rounded rear edge of the anal fin. *Size:* Length to 25.5 inches (65 cm). *Range and Habitat:* Amchitka Island, Alaska, to Huntington Beach, California. Formerly were usually in large aggregations around rocky reefs and over soft bottoms; from the surface to 1200 ft (367 m). *Natural History:* Black rockfish feed on a variety of fishes, molluscs, and crustaceans. Black rockfish are sought by both sport anglers, and commercial fishers. The population is considered depleted.

Adult

49. BLUE ROCKFISH   *Sebastes mystinus*

Identification: The blue rockfish can be separated from the dusky rockfish (#50) by the lighter gray-blue mottling on the sides and the weak or absent symphyseal knob. *Size:* Length to 21 inches (53 cm). *Range and Habitat:* Bering Sea to Punta Banda, Baja California. Around shallow rocky reefs; from surface to 1,800 ft (549 m). *Natural History:* Blue rockfish feed on a variety of the larger planktonic animals, including jellyfish and salps. At one time the blue rockfish was one of the most common species captured by sport anglers fishing from skiffs and party boats off central California. Overfishing caused declines in the population, so this is no longer true.

50. DUSKY ROCKFISH   *Sebastes ciliatus*

Identification: The moderate symphyseal knob and greenish-brown body usually will separate the dusky rockfish from the blue rockfish (#49). *Size:* Length to 16 inches (41 cm). *Range and Habitat:* Bering Sea and Gulf of Alaska to Johnstone Strait, British Columbia; around rocky reefs; in depths to 1,750 ft (525 m). *Natural History:* In Alaska, the dusky and black rockfish are usually found near the same rock piles. Their food consists primarily of zooplankton.

51. SQUARESPOT ROCKFISH
Sebastes hopkinsi

Identification: The long, second, anal fin spine, which extends beyond the tip of the third spine, and the dark blotches on and above the lateral line will separate the squarespot rockfish from the widow (#52), yellowtail (#53), and olive (#54) rockfishes. *Size:* Length to 11.5 inches (29 cm). *Range and Habitat:* Cape Blanco, Oregon, to Guadalupe Island, Baja California. Around deep reefs; from 60 to 600 ft (18 to 183 m).

52. WIDOW ROCKFISH *Sebastes entomelas*

Identification: Widow rockfish have black membranes between the rays in the anal, pectoral, and pelvic fins. Their maxillary does not reach beyond the middle of the eye. *Size:* Length to 21 inches (53 cm). *Range and Habitat:* Kodiak Island, Alaska, to Todos Santos Bay, Baja California. Around offshore reefs and in midwater; in depths to 1,250 ft (375 m). *Natural History:* Widow rockfish occur in very large aggregations in midwater where they feed on plankton.

53. YELLOWTAIL ROCKFISH
Sebastes flavidus

Identification: The yellowtail rockfish can usually be separated from its look-alike, the olive rockfish (#54), by the yellow areas on the gill cover, light orange-brown speckles on body scales, and eight soft rays in the anal fin. *Size:* Length to 26 inches (66 cm). *Range and Habitat:* Unalaska Island, Alaska, to San Diego, California. Around offshore reefs; to depths of 1800 ft (549 m). *Natural History:* Based on tagging studies, yellowtail rockfish have a homing instinct and will return to the reef where they were originally caught if given the opportunity. This species can live to at least age 20. The population is probably depleted.

54. OLIVE ROCKFISH *Sebastes serranoides*

Identification: Olive rockfish usually have nine soft rays in the anal fin and lack the orange-brown speckles on the body scales of the yellowtail rockfish (#53). *Size:* Length to 24 inches (61 cm). *Range and Habitat:* Redding Rock, Humboldt County, California, to San Benito Islands, Baja California. Around reefs and in kelp beds; to depths of 480 ft (146 m). *Natural History:* Food consists mainly of crustaceans, fishes and squid. The oldest fish observed in recent studies was a 14 year old female.

55. PUGET SOUND ROCKFISH
Sebastes emphaeus

Identification: Underwater, the faded colors of the copper-red body with greenish-brown bars and blotches are distinctive. *Size:* Length to 7 inches (18 cm). *Range and Habitat:* Prince William Sound, Alaska, to Punta Gorda, Baja California. Around reefs; from 35 to over 1,200 ft (11 to 366 m). *Natural History:* Females are mature at about 6 inches (15 cm) in length; the larvae are released by the female in the late summer. These small rockfish feed on midwater and surface zooplankton.

56. CANARY ROCKFISH *Sebastes pinniger*

Identification: Canary rockfish lack rough scales on the underside of the jaw (mandible) and the body is yellow-orange and gray in color. Fish smaller than 1.2 ft (36 cm) have a large, black blotch on the spinous dorsal fin. *Size:* Length to 30 inches (76 cm). *Range and Habitat:* Cape San Bartolome, Alaska, to Cape Colnett, Baja California. Around reefs and over soft bottoms; to depths of 1,417 ft (425 m). *Natural History:* A 2l-to 26-inch (53-to 66-cm) female may produce up to l,900,000 larval rockfish. Canary rockfish can live at least to 13 years of age. Commercially, the population of this once important fish is depleted. They feed on crustaceans and fishes.

Juvenile
Adult

Juvenile

57. VERMILION ROCKFISH
Sebastes miniatus

Identification: Differs from the other shallow water "red" rockfishes, the canary (#56) and yelloweye (#58), by having rough scales on the underside of jaw and mottled gray background on body. *Size:* Length to 30 inches (76 cm). *Range and Habitat:* Prince William Sound, Alaska, to San Benito Islands, Baja California. Around reefs; in depths to 900 ft (275 m). *Natural History:* Female vermilion rockfish can live to at least age 29. Females begin sexual maturity at about age 4. Food consists of crustaceans, fishes, squid and octopuses.

45

Adult vermilion rockfish
Juvenile

Adult

58. YELLOWEYE ROCKFISH
Sebastes ruberrimus

Identification: The yellow eye, flattened, rasp-like spines on the head of the adults, and lack of scales on the jaw or on the maxillary are good distinguishing characteristics. *Size:* Length to 3 ft (91 cm). *Range and Habitat:* Unman Island, Alaska, to Ensenada, Baja California. Around reefs where there are plenty of caves and crevices; in depths from about 50 to 1,800 ft (15 to 549 m). *Natural History:* This large solitary fish may live as long as 100 years. In a recent study a 24 inch (61 cm) female was aged at 23 years. Females do not reach sexual maturity until they are at least 16 inches (40 cm) and 10 years old.

46

59. KELP ROCKFISH *Sebastes atrovirens*

Identification: Often confused with the grass rockfish (#60), but gill rakers on the first arch are long and slender, not short and stubby. *Size:* Length to l6.75 inches (42 cm). *Range and Habitat:* Timber Cove, California, to Punta San Pablo, Baja California Sur. Primarily in kelp forests; solitary fish usually observed off bottom near kelp in depths to l50 ft (46m). *Natural History:* Female kelp rockfish reach sexual maturity beginning at age 5 (8.5 inches, 21.5 cm). Their food consists of a variety of crustaceans, fishes and molluscs.

60. GRASS ROCKFISH *Sebastes rastrelliger*

Identification: Differs from the kelp rockfish (#59) by the dark olive-green mottling on the head and body and the 22 to 25 short, stubby gill rakers on the first gill arch (the only rockfish having this type of gill rakers). *Size:* Length to 22 inches (56 cm). *Range and Habitat:* Yaquina Bay, Oregon, to Playa Maria Bay, Baja California. Around eel grass beds and rocky areas with crevices; intertidal out to l50 ft (46 m). *Natural History:* Grass rockfish feed on fishes and crabs. Live to at least age 20. Sexual maturity in females begins at age 5 (l2.75 inches, 32.4 cm).

6l. BROWN ROCKFISH *Sebastes auriculatus*

Identification: The dark brown spot on the rear of the gill cover is very noticeable, also the presence of a coronal spine on the head is a good character if you have the fish in hand. *Size:* Length to 2l.5 inches (55 cm). *Range and Habitat:* Prince William Sound, Alaska, to Hipolito Bay, Baja California Sur. Around low profile reefs in sandy or silty areas; to depths of 420 ft (l28 m). *Natural History:* Females begin maturing at about 11.5 inches (29.2 cm).

62. QUILLBACK ROCKFISH
Sebastes maliger

Identification: Quillback rockfish can be readily recognized by the brown and yellow body color, the brown spots on the anterior ventral portion of the body, and the spinous dorsal fin with deeply notched membranes. *Size:* Length to 24 inches (6l cm). *Range and Habitat:* Gulf of Alaska to San Miguel Island, California. In and around off-shore rocky reefs that contain caves and crevices; in depths of about 30 to 900 ft (9 to 274 m). *Natural History:* A valued sport and commercial species in British Columbia.

Juvenile

63 CHINA ROCKFISH *Sebastes nebulosus*

Identification: The yellow stripe that runs from the front part of the spiny dorsal fin down to the lateral line then posteriorly to the base of the cau-dal fin, and the whitish or yellow spots are good identification characters. *Size:* Length to l7.8 inches (45.3 cm). *Range and Habitat:* Prince William Sound, Alaska to Redondo Beach, Cali-fornia. In and around offshore reefs, with crev-ices and caves; in depths from l0 to 420 ft (3 to l28 m). *Natural History:* China rockfish feed on crustaceans, brittle stars and molluscs. These at-tractive and tasty rockfish can live to at least 26 years. Females begin maturing at about l0.5 inches (26.2 cm).

Adult

64. BLACK-AND-YELLOW ROCKFISH
Sebastes chrysomelas

Identification: The black-and-yellow rockfish is indistinguishable from the gopher rockfish (#65), except for the color pattern of large yellow to orange blotches on a black body. Also, the lower lip is gray, not orange or yellow. *Size:* Length to l5.25 inches (39 cm). *Range and Habitat:* Eureka, California, to Natividad Island, Baja California Sur; around shallow rocky reefs; to depths of l20 ft (37 m). *Natural History:* In recent studies a male black-and-yellow rockfish was aged at 2l years. Females begin maturing at 6 years (9.5 inches, 24.3 cm). These fish feed on a variety of crustaceans, molluscs and fishes.

65. GOPHER ROCKFISH *Sebastes carnatus*

Identification: Gopher rockfish, in contrast to black-and-yellow rockfishes (#64), have flesh-colored spots and blotches on an olive-brown to brown body. Their lower lip is orange and the soft dorsal fin is dark olive in color. *Size:* Length to 15.6 inches (40 cm). *Range and Habitat:* Eureka, California, to San Roque, Baja California Sur; in and around rocky reefs with caves and crevices; in depths from 10 to 180 ft (3 to 55 m). *Natural History:* These territorial rockfish reach at least 24 years in age. Females start becoming sexually mature at about 8 inches (20.5 cm). Gopher rockfish feed on crustaceans, fishes, squid and octopus.

66. COPPER ROCKFISH *Sebastes caurinus*

Identification: The copper-brown body with a white area along the posterior two-thirds of the lateral line readily separates the copper rockfish from the brown rockfish (#6l), as does the lack of a coronal spine. The soft dorsal fin is creamy white in color. *Size:* Length to 22.5 inches (57 cm). *Range and Habitat:* Kenai Peninsula, Alaska, to San Benito Islands, Baja California. Around offshore rocky reefs; from shallow bays to 600 ft (183 m). *Natural History:* Feed on crabs, shrimps and fishes. Copper rockfish live to at least 28 years of age. Sexual maturity in females begins at about 11.5 inches (29.5 cm).

67. CALICO ROCKFISH — *Sebastes dalli*

Identification: The calico rockfish can be readily recognized by the slanting brown bars on the light yellow to yellow-green body. *Size:* Length to l0 inches (25 cm). *Range and Habitat:* San Francisco, California, to Rompiente Point, Baja California Sur. Around deeper rocky reefs; from 60 to 840 ft (18 to 256 m).

68. HONEYCOMB ROCKFISH — *Sebastes umbrosus*

Identification: The honeycomb rockfish has distinctive blackish margins on the scales forming a honeycomb pattern, white blotches on the back, and white edges on the dorsal, caudal, and anal fins. They differ from the deep water freckled rockfish *S. lentiginosus* (not illustrated) in not having tooth knobs on the premaxillary bones. *Size:* Length to 10.5 inches (27 cm); *S. lentiginosus* to 9 inches (23 cm). *Range and Habitat: S. umbrosus:* Pt. Pinos, Monterey County, California, to Pt. San Juanico, Baja California; *S. lentiginosus:* Santa Catalina Island to Los Coronados, Baja California; around bases of offshore rocky reefs; in depths of 90 to 390 ft (27 to 119 m), and l30 to 550 ft (40 to 168 m) respectively.

69. ROSY ROCKFISH — *Sebastes rosaceus*

Identification: The four or five white blotches on the back have purplish-red borders; this character and the purple bar across the nape will separate the rosy rockfish from the less common, deep-water rosethorn rockfish *S. helvomaculatus* (not illustrated). The rosethorn rockfish has only 16 pectoral rays; the rosy rockfish has 17. *Size: S. rosaceus:* length to 14.2 inches (36 cm); *S. helvomaculatus* to 16 inches (4l cm). *Range and Habitat: S. rosaceus:* Cobb Seamount, North Pacific, to Turtle Bay, Baja California Sur; *S. helvomaculatus:* Kodiak Island to Point Loma, California. Around offshore rocky reefs, usually in caves or crevices. In depths of 50 to 469 ft (15 to 143 m) and 438 to 1,500 ft (134 to 458 m) respectively. *Natural History:* These solitary rockfish reach at least age 14. Females reach sexual maturity beginning at about 9.5 inches (245 mm).

70. STARRY ROCKFISH
Sebastes constellatus

Identification: Good identification characters are four or five whitish blotches on the back and numerous small white spots covering the body. *Size:* Length to 18 inches (46 cm). *Range and Habitat:* Punta Gorda, California, to Thetis Bank, Baja California Sur. Around offshore rocky reefs with caves and crevices; in depths of 65 to 900 ft (20 to 274 m). *Natural History:* Maximum age observed in a recent study was 19 years, 17.25 inches (442 mm). Sexual maturity in females begins at age 7 (10.75 inches 270 mm).

71. HALFBANDED ROCKFISH
Sebastes semicinctus

Identification: Halfbanded rockfish have two diamond shaped, dark bars on each side, one beneath the spiny dorsal fin and the other below the soft rayed dorsal fin. The brownish spots on the back and dorsal fin are very distinctive even in younger fish. *Size:* Length to 10 inches (25 cm). *Range and Habitat:* Monterey Bay, California to Sebastian Vizcaino Bay, Baja California; around rocky areas and over soft bottoms. Adults are found in depths of 190 to 1320 ft (58 to 402 m); young fish occur in depths as shallow at 50 ft (15 m) during their first year of life.

72. STRIPETAIL ROCKFISH
Sebastes saxicola

Identification: Young stripetail rockfish have two bars on their side, one below the rear of the spiny dorsal fin and one below the soft rayed portion of the dorsal fin. Adults and young have green stripes on the caudal fin. *Size:* Length to 15.3 inches (39 cm). *Range and Habitat:* Southeastern Alaska to Sebastian Vizcaino Bay, Baja California; on soft bottoms and around reefs. Adults found in deep water, 150 to 1380 ft (46 to 421 m); juveniles are found in shallower water. *Natural History:* Some of these small rockfish are mature at age 2 (5 inches 12.7 cm) but most males and females don't become mature until after age 4.

73. TIGER ROCKFISH *Sebastes nigrocinctus*
Identification: The distinctive body color of light pink to red, with five vertical, dark red to black bars, separate this rockfish from all others. *Size:* Length to 24 inches (61 cm). *Range and Habitat:* Prince William Sound, Alaska, to Point Buchon, California. In crevices and caves; in depths from about 80 to 900 ft (24 to 274 m). *Natural History:* Tiger rockfish are very cryptic and usually are shy around divers; however, they can be very aggressive in defending their territory.

74. TREEFISH *Sebastes serriceps*
Identification: The treefish is best identified by the 5 to 6 black bars on the olive-yellow body and the red lips. *Size:* Length to 16 inches (41 cm). *Range and Habitat:* San Francisco, California, to Cedros Island, Baja California. Around rocky reefs with caves and crevices; from shallow depths to 150 ft (46 m). *Natural History:* Treefish are solitary rockfish and are not commonly caught by anglers. They are one of the more common reef fishes encountered by divers in Southern California.

75. FLAG ROCKFISH *Sebastes rubrivinctus*
Identification: Flag rockfish are often confused with the deep water redbanded rockfish *S. babcocki (*not illustrated), but there is a difference in the vertical red bands. *S. rubrivinctus'* first band angles anteriorly from the first dorsal spine down across the rear of the gill cover, while the band on *S. babcocki* angles posteriorly across the upper edge of the gill cover and ends on the pectoral fin. *Size: S. rubrivinctus:* Length to 20 inches (51 cm). *S babcocki:* length to 25 inches (64 cm). *Range and Habitat: S. rubrivinctus:* San Francisco, California, to San Quintin, Baja California. *S. babcocki:* Amchitka, Alaska, to San Diego, California. Around offshore reefs; from 100 to 600 ft (31 to 183 m), and 900 to 1,560 ft (274 to 476 m), respectively.

FAMILY ANOPLOPOMATIDAE
Sablefishes

Sablefishes have two dorsal fins and small scales. The thoracic pelvic fins have one spine and five soft rays. There are only two family members; both occur in the cold northern Pacific waters.

76. SABLEFISH   *Anoplopoma fimbria*
Identification: Sablefish have two dorsal fins with a wide space in between. The first dorsal is composed of 17 to 30 spines and the second has 16 to 21 soft rays. The second dorsal fin is located immediately above the anal fin. *Size:* Length to 3.3 ft (1 m). *Range and Habitat:* Japan and Bering Sea to Cedros Island, Baja California. Adults in deep water, l000 to 5000 ft (305 to l,524 m), over soft bottoms. Young fish often occur near shore in shallower depths. *Natural History:* Tagging studies indicate that these very important commercial fish perform extensive migrations. They feed on other fish, crustaceans and worms.

FAMILY HEXAGRAMMIDAE
Greenlings and Lingcod

Members of this family have a single dorsal fin composed of spines and soft rays. They are related to the rockfishes and sculpins, but lack spines on the head. Most species have more than one lateral line. Ten species have been recorded, all from the North Pacific.

Male
Female

77. KELP GREENLING
Hexagrammos decagrammus

Identification: Kelp greenlings have two pairs of cirri, one over the eyes and the other, smaller pair is located between the eyes and the origin of the dorsal fin (occasionally the second pair is absent). The cirri over the eyes are never more than ∫ the diameter of the eye. The interior of the mouth is usually yellowish. *Size:* Length to 21 inches (53 cm). *Range and Habitat:* Aleutian Islands, Alaska, to La Jolla, California. Around rocky reefs and in kelp beds; from the intertidal to 150 ft (46 m). *Natural History:* Spawning takes place in the fall and the males guard the egg masses until they hatch. Young kelp greenlings are fed on by salmon.

B. Hanby

78. WHITESPOTTED GREENLING
Hexagrammos stelleri

Identification: The white spots, single pair of cirri over eyes, and the short fourth lateral line, which does not extend posteriorly beyond origin of the anal fin, are all good characters for identifying this fish. *Size:* Length to 19 inches (48 cm). *Range and Habitat:* Japan to Puget Sound, Washington. Around shallow reefs and kelp beds. From shallow water to 150 ft (46 m). *Natural History:* These uncommonly observed greenlings feed on worms, crustaceans, and small fishes. Spawning takes place in April.

79. ROCK GREENLING
Hexagrammos superciliosus

Identification: Rock greenlings have blue mouths and a single pair of large cirri over the eyes; each cirrus will be more than ∫ diameter of eye. *Size:* Length to 24 inches (6l cm). *Range and Habitat:* Bering Sea to Point Conception, California; around very shallow, rocky reefs and kelp beds. *Natural History:* These beautiful fish are caught by shore anglers, but are rarely observed by divers.

Visuals Unlimited/G. Oliver

80. PAINTED GREENLING *Oxylebius pictus*

Identification: Painted greenling possess only one lateral line and 2 pairs of cirri. They differ from the other members of the family in having a very small mouth; the end of the maxillary does not reach the eye. Color variable. *Size:* Length to 10 inches (25 cm). *Range and Habitat:* Kodiak Island, Alaska, to San Benito Islands, Baja California; around rocky reefs; from the intertidal to depths of l60 ft (49 m). *Natural History:* During the spawning season the males' body coloration becomes very dark, almost black, with white spots.

81. LINGCOD
Ophiodon elongatus

Identification: Lingcod have only one lateral line and they are the only member of the family that has a large mouth and large canine teeth; the maxillary extends to at least the middle of the eye. *Size:* Length to 5 ft (l52 cm), weight to 105 lb (48 kg). *Range and Habitat:* Shumagin Islands and Prince William Sound, Alaska, to Point San Carlos, Baja California. Around rock reefs, juveniles on sand and mud bottom; from shallow bays to depths of l,583 ft (475 m). *Natural History:* Males guard eggs until they hatch; lingcod feed on fishes, squids, and octopus. Lingcod are highly esteemed by sport anglers as well as commercial fishers. But due to overfishing the harvesting of this fish by both groups has been severely restricted.

82. LONGSPINE COMBFISH
Zaniolepis latipinnis

Identification: The three very long dorsal spines (the second spine longer than the third) distinguish this family member from all the others. *Size:* Length to 12 inches (30 cm). *Range and Habitat:* Vancouver Island, British Columbia, to Central Baja California on soft bottoms, 70 to 660 ft (21 to 201 m). *Natural History:* Commonly caught and usually discarded by commercial trawlers. When captured they assume a trance-like behavior and horseshoe-shape.

N. McDaniel

FAMILY COTTIDAE
Sculpins

Cottids, like rockfishes and greenlings, have a suborbital stay (bony connection under the cheek). Most species have large heads, round bodies, 1 to 4 preopercular spines (on the anterior part of the gill cover) and large, fan-like pectoral fins. A microscope is needed to identify many of the species.

The members of this large family are mostly limited to the temperate marine and freshwater waters of the northern hemisphere; a few species are in the southern hemisphere.

There are about 300 recognized species; 230 of which are marine fishes. There are 85 species off our coast.

83. CORALLINE SCULPIN
Artedius corallinus

Identification: The members of this genus are almost impossible to separate underwater. Very similar to *Artedius lateralis,* the smoothhead sculpin (#84). The only way to separate the two is by examination with a hand lens; the coralline sculpin has 39 to 49 oblique rows of scales, with 10 to 18 scales in longest row. *Size:* Length to 5.5 inches (14 cm). *Range and Habitat:* Orcas Island, Washington, to San Martin Island, Baja California. Around rocky reefs; in depths from intertidal to 70 ft (21 m). *Natural History:* One of the most commonly observed sculpins in central California.

56

84. SMOOTHHEAD SCULPIN

Artedius lateralis

Identification: The smoothhead sculpin has only 18 to 29 oblique rows of scales, 3 to 11 scales in the longest row. All fins except pelvics have bars. *Size:* Length to 5.5 inches (14 cm). *Range and Habitat:* Kodiak Island, Alaska, to northern Baja California. Common in tidepools, but also occurs in bays and near shore waters to 43 ft (13 m). *Natural History:* Smoothhead sculpins feed on other sculpins, and crabs. Spawning occurs in February in British Columbia.

85. SCALYHEAD SCULPIN

Artedius harringtoni

Identification: The scalyhead sculpin has scales on the head, occasionally on cheeks, but never on the snout. For complete description see *A Field Guide to Pacific Coast Fishes of North America* by Eschmeyer, Herald, and Hammer. The scalyhead sculpin is one of the most common sculpins observed by divers from northern California to British Columbia. *Size:* Length to 4 inches (10 cm). *Range and Habitat:* Kodiak Island, Alaska, to San Miguel Island, California; intertidal rocky areas to reefs as deep as 70 ft (21 m).

G. Jensen

86. SILVERSPOTTED SCULPIN

Blepsias cirrhosus

Identification: This sculpin has prominent cirri on the snout and lower jaw and a high spinous first dorsal fin with a distinctive notch. There are white and silver marks on the sides near the pectoral fin. The brown to black fins have large clear areas. *Size:* Length to 7.5 inches (19 cm). *Range and Habitat:* Sea of Japan and Bering Sea to San Simeon, California; among algae, rocky intertidal to 120 ft (37 m). *Natural History:* Spawning takes place in the late winter. The eggs are attached to rocks.

57

G. Jensen

87. ROUGHBACK SCULPIN
Chitonotus pugetensis

Identification: The first dorsal fin spine of this sculpin is very long, almost twice the length of the second spine. Also, there is a deep notch between the third and fourth dorsal fin spines. *Size:* Length to 9 inches (23 cm). *Range and Habitat:* Ucluelet, British Columbia, Canada, to Santa Maria Bay, Baja California, Mexico; on soft bottoms, intertidal to 466 ft (142 m). *Natural History:* These deeper water sculpins feed on shrimps and other small crustaceans.

88. BUFFALO SCULPIN   *Enophrys bison*

Identification: Buffalo sculpins have a single long preopercular spine, bony plates on the lateral line, and 8 to 10 soft rays in the anal fin. Buffalo sculpin can be confused with the less common bull sculpin (*E. taurina,* not illustrated) which have only 6 to 7 soft-rays in the anal fin. *Size: E. bison:* length to 14.5 inches (37 cm); *E. taurina:* length to 6.8 inches (17 cm). *Range and Habitat: E. bison:* Kodiak Island, Alaska, to Monterey Bay, California. *E. taurina:* San Francisco, California, to Santa Catalina Island, California. Both species are found on rocky and soft bottoms to depths of 65 ft (20 m) and 840 ft (256 m), respectively.

89. RED IRISH LORD
Hemilepidotus hemilepidotus

Identification: Red Irish lords have only four or five rows of scales below the dorsal fin and several patches of red on the upper body. *Size:* Length to 20 inches (51 cm). *Range and Habitat:* Sea of Okhotsk to Monterey Bay, California. On rocky reefs; in depths from the intertidal to 158 ft (48 m). *Natural History:* Red Irish lords feed on crabs, barnacles and mussels. Spawning takes place in the spring.

90. BROWN IRISH LORD
Hemilepidotus spinosus

Identification: Brown Irish lords are very difficult to distinguish from the red Irish lord (#89) underwater. If you have the fish in hand, count the scale rows below the dorsal fin. If it has seven to eight rows, it is a brown Irish lord. *Size:* Length to 11.3 inches (29 cm). *Range and Habitat:* Prince William Sound, Alaska, to Santa Barbara Island, California. Around reefs; from the intertidal to depths of 318 ft (97 m). *Natural History:* These cryptic sculpins feed on a variety of crustaceans such as small crabs of the genus *Cancer*.

P. Edgell

G. Jensen

91. NORTHERN SCULPIN *Icelinus borealis*

Identification: This uncommon sculpin has two rows of scales below the dorsal fin that extend onto the caudal peduncle. *Size:* Length to 4 inches (10 cm). *Range and Habitat:* Bering Sea to Puget Sound, Washington, on soft bottoms from 30 to 700 ft (9.1 to 213 m). *Natural History:* Usually caught in locations where large concentrations of shrimp, its prey, are found.

92. PITHEAD SCULPIN *Icelinus cavifrons*

Identification: The double row of scales below the dorsal fins does not extend beyond the posterior of the second dorsal fin. There is a distinctive pit on the top of the head behind the eyes. The base of the pectoral fins is black. *Size:* Length to 3.5 inches (8.9 cm). *Range and Habitat:* Monterey Bay, California, to Guadalupe Island, Baja California. On soft bottoms and low profile reefs in depths of 36 to 300 ft (11 to 91 m).

93. THREADFIN SCULPIN
Icelinus filamentosus
Identification: The first two dorsal spines of this sculpin are thread-like and are both longer than the rest of the spines. *Size:* Length to 10.6 inches (27 cm). *Range and Habitat:* Northern British Columbia to Cortez Bank off southern California; on sand and mud bottoms, sometimes on or around low profile reefs. *Natural History:* Threadfin sculpins feed on shrimp and other crustaceans.

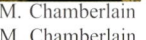

M. Chamberlain
M. Chamberlain

94. SPOTFIN SCULPIN   *Icelinus tenuis*
Identification: Differs from the threadfin sculpin (#93) in that the first very elongate dorsal fin spine is longer than the second and about 2 times longer than the rest of the spines. *Size:* Length to 5.5 inches (14 cm). *Range and Habitat:* Queen Charlotte Islands, British Columbia, to San Benito Islands, Baja California; on sandy bottoms occasionally near reefs in depths of about 90 to 1224 ft (28 to 373 m).

95. LONGFIN SCULPIN   *Jordania zonope*
Identification: The only slender sculpin in our area with three black vertical bars below the eye and 17 to 18 spines in the dorsal fin. Scales present on most of body above lateral line. *Size:* Length to 6 inches (15 cm). *Range and Habitat:* Prince William Sound, Alaska, to Avila, California. In and around caves and crevices; from the intertidal to 126 ft (38 m). *Natural History:* In British Columbia spawning takes place in October.

96. LAVENDER SCULPIN

Leiocottus hirundo

Identification: The distinctive blue spots on the dorsal fin, red bands on the sides of the body, and the long first dorsal spine, which is about twice as long as the third dorsal spine, separate this fish from other sculpins. *Size:* Length to 10 inches (25 cm). *Range and Habitat:* Point Conception, California, to Punta Banda, Baja California. On sand and rock bottoms around kelp beds; in depths from intertidal to 120 ft (37 m).

97. PACIFIC STAGHORN SCULPIN

Leptocottus armatus

Identification: Pacific staghorn sculpins lack scales. They have a long antlerlike spine on the upper preopercle. There is a dark spot at the rear of the first dorsal fin. *Size:* Length to 18 inches (46 cm). *Range and Habitat:* Southern Bering Sea to San Quintin Bay, Baja California. Found on soft bottoms in bays and offshore; intertidal to 3000 ft (914 m). *Natural History:* These sculpins are important bait fish in San Francisco Bay. They are sexually mature at age one and spawn during the fall and winter. Pacific staghorn sculpins feed on a variety of fishes, crustaceans, worms and molluscs.

98. GREAT SCULPIN

Myoxocephalus polyacanthocephalus

Identification: There are at least three species of *Myoxocephalus*. The great sculpin is apparently the largest and possesses a long, straight, smooth upper opercular spine and scales embedded in fleshy papillae on head. The mouth is large, with a maxillary that extends to the rear edge of the eye. *Size:* Length to 30 inches (76 cm). *Range and Habitat:* Japan and Bering Sea to Washington. On soft bottoms and around reefs; from the intertidal to depths of 800 ft (244 m). *Natural History:* These large sculpins feed on other fish.

99. SAILFIN SCULPIN
Nautichthys oculofasciatus

Identification: This nocturnal sculpin is readily identified by the high spinous dorsal fin and the dark vertical band that runs through the eye. *Size:* Length to 8 inches (20 cm). *Range and Habitat:* Eastern Kamchatka and Prince William Sound, Alaska, to San Miguel Island, California. Around rocky reefs; from the intertidal to depths of 360 ft (110 m). *Natural History:* Spawning takes place in late winter and early spring. Sailfin sculpins feed on crustaceans.

G. Jensen

100. ROSYLIP SCULPIN
Ascelichthys rhodorus

Identification: This sculpin lacks pelvic fins and scales. There is a branched cirrus above each eye. The lips and edge of the dorsal fin are often red. *Size:* Length to about 6 inches (15 cm). *Range and Habitat:* Sitka, Alaska to Pillar Point, California, rocky intertidal and shallow subtidal.

101. SNUBNOSE SCULPIN
Orthonopias triacis

Identification: The snubnose and the location of the anus much closer to the base of the pelvic fins than to the anal fin separates this common sculpin from all others. *Size:* Length to 4 inches (10 cm). *Range and Habitat:* Farallon Islands, California, to San Geronimo Island, Baja California. Around rocky areas; intertidal to depths of 100 ft (30 m).

102. TADPOLE SCULPIN
Psychrolutes paradoxus

Identification: The large, smooth head and tadpolelike shape; scaleless body, except for two rows of small prickles on belly; and the lack of cirri and spines on the preopercle are distinctive. *Size:* Length to 2.5 inches (6.8 cm). *Range and Habitat:* Northern Sea of Japan; Sea of Okhotsk and Bering Sea to Puget Sound; on soft bottoms, occasionally rocky areas to depths of 30 to 720 ft (9.l to 219 m). *Natural History:* Young tadpole sculpins are known to feed on small crustaceans.

G. Jensen
G. Jensen

103. SPINYNOSE SCULPIN
Asemichthys taylori

Identification: The long pectoral fins, slender, slightly flattened body and one row of scales above the lateral line are distinctive. The length of the short snout is equal to or less than the diameter of the eye. *Size:* Length to 3 inches (7.6 cm). *Range and Habitat:* Southeastern Alaska to Straits of Georgia, Washington; on shell and cobble bottoms, 20 to 60 ft (6.1 to 18 m).

104. GRUNT SCULPIN
Rhamphocottus richardsonii

Identification: This distinctive, deep bodied sculpin can be identified by the snout, about twice the length of the maxillary; and the free, lower-most pectoral rays, and its tank-like appearance. *Size:* Length to 3.25 inches (8.3 cm). *Range and Habitat:* Japan and Bering Sea to Santa Monica Bay, California. On rocky reefs; from the inter-tidal to depths of 540 ft (165 m). *Natural History:* Grunt sculpins often "walk" about using their large pectoral fins. They feed on crustaceans. When removed from water they often make grunting sounds.

105. CABEZON *Scorpaenichthys marmoratus*
Identification: Cabezon have no scales on their bodies; they have a large cirrus over each eye, and a single cirrus on the snout. *Size:* Length to 3.1 ft (1.0 m). *Range and Habitat:* Sitka, Alaska, to Point Abreojos, Baja California Sur. Around rocky reefs; from the intertidal to depths of 250 ft (75 m). *Natural History:* Feed on molluscs, such as squids, octopus, and abalone, and crabs; males guard eggs. They are highly sought after by sport anglers who fish rocky shores. Their roe is poisonous.

R. Borema

106. MANACLED SCULPIN *Synchirus gilli*
Identification: This sculpin is the only member of the family that has pectoral fins that are joined across the breast. There is only one two-pointed spine on the preopercle. *Size:* Length to 2.75 inches (7 cm). *Range and Habitat:* Sitka, Alaska, to San Miguel Island, California. In kelp beds, shallow bays, and tidepools. *Natural History:* These sculpins use their modified pectoral fins to cling to kelp, pilings and other objects. Manacled sculpins feed on small crustaceans.

FAMILY AGONIDAE
Poachers

Poachers have modified rows of scales that are fused into bony plates, which usually have spines. In most cases there are two dorsal fins, the first fin composed of spines and the second composed of soft rays. Their pectoral fins are fanlike. There are no spines in the anal fin. The anal fin is usually larger in males.

The members of this family have been recorded from the North Pacific and North Atlantic; one species is found off the southern tip of South America. Of the 50 known species 21 have been reported from this coast.

107. KELP POACHER *Agonamalus mozinoi*

Identification: The red and brown coloration readily distinguishes this poacher. There are rows of spines on the sides of the body and a long skin flap on the snout. *Size:* Length to 3.5 inches (8.9 cm). *Range and Habitat:* Dixon Entrance, British Columbia, to San Simeon, California, on shallow rocky areas to depths of 35 ft (11 m). *Natural History:* The body is often covered with sponges and seaweed, which afford camouflage. Uses pectoral fins to crawl about.

G. Jensen

108. SOUTHERN SPEARNOSE POACHER
Agonopsis sterletus

Identification: Southern spearnose poachers are similar in appearance to northern spearnose poachers (#109), but lack the cirri below the rostral spines on the snout. The southern spearnose poacher has dark brown pelvic fins with white tips, while the northern spearnose poacher has white pelvic fins. *Size:* Length to 5.8 inches (15 cm). *Range and Habitat:* San Simeon, Califonia, to Point San Hippolito, Baja California Sur; on soft bottoms, in bays, and open ocean to depths of 300 ft (91 m). *Natural History:* Most poachers feed on small crustaceans. They form part of the discarded by-catch of commercial trawlers.

G. Jensen

109. NORTHERN SPEARNOSE POACHER
Agonopsis vulsa

Identification: There are cirri under the pointed snout, and the rear of the head has a pit. The anal fin begins below the first dorsal fin; the pelvic fins are dark in color. *Size:* Length to 8 inches (20 cm). *Range and Habitat:* Bering Sea to Eureka, California. On soft and cobble bottoms, 60 to 534 ft (18 to 163 m).

110. STURGEON POACHER

Agonus acipenserinus

Identification: The sturgeon poacher is the only poacher with clusters of yellow cirri under the snout and mouth corners. The mouth is on the underside of the head. *Size:* Length to 12 inches (30 m). *Range and Habitat:* Bering Sea to Eureka, California. On soft bottoms and around reefs; in depths from about 10 to 180 ft (3 to 55 m). *Natural History:* Sturgeon poachers feed on crustaceans and worms.

G. Jensen

111. ROCKHEAD   *Bothragonus swanii*

Identification: The body is deep and the bony plates are large and smooth. The anal and dorsal fins are small. No more than five rays in each fin. There is a deep pit in the top of the head. *Size:* Length to 3.5 inches (8.9 cm). *Range and Habitat:* Kodiak Island, Alaska, to Lion Rock, California; rocky bottoms from intertidal to 60 ft (18 m).

G. Jensen

112. FOURHORN POACHER

Hypsagonus quadricornis

Identification: This deep bodied poacher has a spine above each eye, and the lower rays of the pectoral fin are free of the membrane. There is a prominent cirrus on the tip of the snout. *Size:* Length to 3.5 inches (8.9 cm). *Range and Habitat:* Sea of Okhotsk and Bering Sea to Puget Sound, Washington. On rocky and soft bottoms, to 730 ft (223 m).

113. PIGMY POACHER
Odontopyxis trispinosa

Identification: There is one spine at the tip of the snout, and a pit at the rear of the head. *Size:* Length to 3.75 inches (9.5 cm). *Range and Habitat:* Southeastern Alaska to Cedros Island, Baja California; on soft bottoms and low profile reefs, 30 to 1224 ft (9 to 373 m). *Natural History:* Pigmy poachers feed on crustaceans.

G. Jensen

114. TUBENOSE POACHER
Pallasina barbata

Identification: This poacher has a long, slender and smooth body and a long snout. The lower jaw projects beyond the upper and there is a barbel at the tip. *Size:* Length to about 5.75 inches (14 cm). *Range and Habitat:* Japan and Bering Sea to Bodega Bay, California; on soft and cobble bottoms, in eel grass, intertidal to 180 ft (55 m).

FAMILY CYCLOPTERIDAE
Snail Fishes

The members of this family are difficult to identify. A typical snailfish has a sucking disc formed from modified pectoral fins. The long dorsal and anal fins are often joined to the caudal fin. There are no scales, except for the lumpsuckers. Most snailfishes are found in cold waters of the Northern Hemisphere and Antarctica, but a few occur in deep tropical seas. They occur from intertidal pools to moderate depths. A few have been found in very deep water. About 150 species are known, 50 from this coast.

115. MARBLED SNAILFISH *Liparis dennyi*
Identification: The large gill slits extend down in front of the pectoral fins. The dorsal and anal fins extend onto the caudal fin and there is no distinctive lobe pattern in the front of the dorsal fin. Color pattern varies from spotted, marbled, plain or streaked on an olive background. *Size:* Length to 12 inches (30 cm). *Range and Habitat:* Gulf of Alaska to Washington on soft bottoms to 730 ft (223 m). *Natural History:* Spawning occurs in the winter. This snailfish feeds on crustaceans.

G. Jensen

116. SHOWY SNAILFISH *Liparis pulchellus*
Identification: The unnotched dorsal fin extends onto the caudal fin for most of its length, as does the anal fin. The gill slits end just above the pectoral fin. Color varies from light to dark brown, usually with wavy lines on body; sometimes plain colored or spotted. *Size:* Length to 10 inches (25 cm). *Range and Habitat:* Russia to Bering Sea; to Monterey Bay, California. Found on soft bottoms, 30 to 600 ft (9.1 to 183 m). *Natural History:* These snailfishes feed on crustaceans, worms, other snailfish and even small flatfishes. A 4 inch (10.2) female matures at one year of age and can provide up to about 900 eggs. A 7 inch female carried 9000 eggs. Spawning occurs in the winter and spring.

G. Jensen

117. PACIFIC SPINY LUMPSUCKER
Eumicrotremus orbis
Identification: There are large conical bony plates on most of the body of this lumpsucker. The modified pectoral fins form a very large disc that covers the entire breast. There are two widely separated dorsal fins. *Size:* Length to 5 inches (13 cm). *Range and Habitat:* Kuril Islands off Northern Japan, and Bering Sea to Puget Sound, Washington; on soft and rocky bottoms to 480 ft (140 m). *Natural History:* This lumpsucker spawns in late winter. Females apparently mature at one inch (25 mm).

FAMILY PERCICHTHYIDAE
Temperate Basses

The members of this family have one spine on the gill cover and a forked caudal fin. They are found in both fresh water and marine waters. Of the approximately 40 described species, one is found off our coast.

118. STRIPED BASS   *Morone saxatilis*
Identification: Striped bass have six to nine stripes on each side. The tail fin is forked. *Size:* Length to 4 ft (1.2 m), weight to 90 lbs. (41 kg). *Range and Habitat:* On this coast, Barkeley Sound, British Columbia, to northern Baja California; over soft bottoms and around piers, jetties and reefs, in large rivers, bays, estuaries, and along open beaches. One of the most popular gamefish on both the Pacific and Atlantic coasts. *Natural History:* Striped bass were introduced from the Atlantic Coast in 1879 to San Francisco Bay. These anadromous fish spawn in the spring. They feed on a variety of other fishes.

FAMILY POLYPRIONIDAE
Giant Sea Basses

These large fishes have small ctenoid scales on the head and body. Strong dorsal spines outnumber the dorsal soft rays. The members of this family are found in most of the world's temperate and tropical seas. There is one species that occurs off our coast.

119. GIANT SEA BASS   *Stereolepis gigas*

Identification: Is distinguished by having two spines on the gill cover rather than three as in the other basses. Juveniles and young adults have black spots on the sides. *Size:* Length to 7 ft (2.1 m) and weight to 557 lbs (253 kg). *Range and Habitat:* Humboldt Bay, California, to the Gulf of California; around rocky reefs; in depths from 18 to 150 ft (5 to 46 m). *Natural History:* May live to over 100 years of age; a 435 lb individual was determined to be about 75 years old. Their food consists of a variety of fish, crabs and shrimp. The California population of giant sea bass has made a remarkable recovery since they were protected in the early 1980's. These large fish aggregate in the summer to spawn.

FAMILY SERRANIDAE
Sea Basses and Groupers

Sea basses and groupers usually have robust bodies, large mouths and the caudal fin is usually rounded or square-cut. The anal fin usually has three spines. There are 2 to 3 spines on the gill cover.

The members of this large, commercially important family are found mostly in tropical waters, with a few ranging into colder temperate seas. There are a few freshwater representatives. Sea basses for the most part are hermaphroditic; some species function both as male and female simultaneously, others begin life as females, then transform into males as they grow larger.

There are about 375 species known worldwide; 10 have been recorded off our coast.

120. BROOMTAIL GROUPER
Mycteroperca xenarcha

Identification: The protruding tail fin rays, which give the rear end of the tail fin a notched appearance, are very distinctive. When these groupers are over the reef, the dark blotches on the body are prominent; when over sand bottoms, the entire body color changes to a light grey or tan and the blotches become indistinct. *Size*: Length to about 48 inches (22 cm) and 97 lbs (44 kg). *Range and Habitat:* San Francisco to Gulf of California and Peru; on rocky reefs and sand bottoms to 70 ft (21 m). *Natural History:* As with the giant sea bass, the broomtail grouper population off California has increased since they were fully protected in the early 1980s.

121. KELP BASS   *Paralabrax clathratus*

Identification: The kelp bass has a third dorsal spine that is about the same length as the fourth and fifth spines. The white blotches between the dorsal fin and lateral line are also distinctive. Old fish have orange-yellow chins. *Size:* Length to 28.5 inches (72 cm); weight to 14.5 lbs (6.6 kg). *Range and Habitat:* Columbia River to Magdalena Bay, Baja California Sur. Around reefs and kelp beds; from the surface to depths of 150 ft (46 m). *Natural History:* This non-migratory bass feeds on other fishes, squid, octopus and crustaceans. Spawning takes place from April to fall months.

122. SPOTTED SAND BASS
Paralabrax maculatofasciatus

Identification: The spotted sand bass has black spots on the upper body and the third dorsal fin spine is longer than the fourth or fifth spine. *Size:* Length to 22 inches (56 cm). *Range and Habitat:* Monterey, California, to Mazatlan, Mexico, including the Gulf of California. On sand and around reefs; to depths of 200 ft (61 m). *Natural History:* These bass function first as females, then later in life as males. The females release pelagic eggs during the spring and summer.

123. BARRED SAND BASS
Paralabrax nebulifer

Identification: The barred sand bass is similar to the spotted sand bass, except that barred sand bass lack the black spots on the body. The third dorsal fine spine is longer than the fourth or fifth spine. *Size:* Length to 25.6 inches (65 cm). *Range and Habitat:* Santa Cruz, California, to Magdalena Bay, Baja California Sur. On sand bottoms and around reefs; to depths of 600 ft (183 m). *Natural History:* Barred sand bass feed on fish, crabs, shrimp, clams and squid. Spawning and the release of pelagic eggs take place during spring and summer months.

71

FAMILY PRIACANTHIDAE
Bigeyes

The body is compressed and members of the family have very large eyes. The small scales are rough and the lower jaw projects beyond the upper jaw. These bottom dwelling fishes occur in tropical seas. Of the 12 known species, only one occurs in the cooler waters off our coast.

124. POPEYE CATALUFA
Pseudopriacanthus serrula
Identification: The very large eyes, the deep oval, crimson body, and large pelvic fins readily identify this nocturnal forager. *Size:* Length to 13 inches (33 cm). *Range and Habitat:* Monterey Bay, California, to Gulf of California and Peru; around reefs to depths of 198 ft (60 m). *Natural History:* These nocturnal fish feed on fish and crustaceans. They may live as long as 15 years.

FAMILY APOGONIDAE
Cardinalfishes

Cardinalfishes usually have two dorsal fins, with spines in the anterior fin and the posterior fin composed of soft rays. There are two spines in the anal fin. This family is represented in all of the world's tropical and semi-tropical seas. A few live in brackish as well as fresh water. There are about 200 species; only two occur in the area covered by this guide.

125. GUADALUPE CARDINAL FISH
Apogon guadalupensis

Identification: This is the only cardinal fish recorded from northern Baja California and southern California. It lacks any spots or bars on the body and dorsal fins. *Size:* Length to 5 inches (13 cm). *Range and Habitat:* Santa Catalina, California, to Cabo San Lucas, Baja California. Nocturnal, in crevices and caves during daylight; to depths of at least 100 ft (30 m). *Natural History:* The eggs are brooded in the mouths of males. Guadalupe cardinal fish feed on planktonic crustaceans and small fishes.

FAMILY MALACANTHIDAE
Tilefishes

Tilefishes have a long, continuous dorsal fin with 6 to 8 spines and 13 to 27 soft rays. The lips are fleshy and the caudal fin is lunate or square-cut. The members of the family occur in the temperate and tropical Pacific, Atlantic and Indian Oceans. About 31 species have been described; only one occurs in our area.

126. OCEAN WHITEFISH
Caulolatilus princeps

Identification: Ocean whitefish might be confused with yellowtail, but their long continuous dorsal fin is of a uniform height and they lack the yellow stripe found on the sides of the yellowtail. *Size:* Length to 40 inches (1.0 m). *Range and Habitat:* Vancouver Island, British Columbia, to Peru. On soft bottoms and around reefs; to depths of 300 ft (92 m). *Natural History:* Apparently ocean whitefish are winter spawners. They feed on small shrimp, crabs, octopus, squid and various fishes.

FAMILY CARANGIDAE
Jacks

Jacks are fast swimming fishes with forked caudal fins, narrow caudal peduncles and two spines preceding, but not attached to the anal fin. The lateral line is arched in front. Some species have pointed scutes (plates) on the posterior portion of the lateral line.

The members of the family can be found worldwide in tropical and warmer temperate seas. About 200 species have been described, 12 species have been reported in our area.

K. Mc Donnel

127. GREEN JACK   *Caranx caballus*
Identification: Green jacks have very long pectoral fins and scutes on the posterior portion of the lateral line. *Size:* Length to 15 inches (38 cm). *Range and Habitat:* Morro Bay, California, to Gulf of California and Peru; over soft bottom and around reefs, usually near the surface.

128. YELLOWTAIL   *Seriola lalandi*
Identification: Yellowtails have yellowish fins and a yellow dusky stripe on each side; a darker stripe extends through the eye. There are no scutes on the lateral line. *Size:* Length to 5 ft (1.5 m), weight to 80 lbs (36 kg.). *Range and Habitat:* British Columbia to Chile; found nearly worldwide throughout subtropical seas. Schools occur around kelp beds, offshore islands, and other rocky areas near the surface. A very important gamefish in southern California. *Natural History:* These popular game fish feed on fish, squid and pelagic crabs.

129. JACK MACKEREL
Trachurus symmetricus

Identification: This pelagic schooling jack differs from other species that occur in our area by having a lateral line with a dorsal branch and 40 to 55 enlarged shields on the median lateral line. *Size:* Length to 32 inches (81 cm). *Range and Habitat:* Southeastern Alaska to the Galapagos Islands. In surface waters around reefs and kelp beds and in open ocean; to depths of 600 ft (183 m). *Natural History:* Jack mackerel feed on fishes and pelagic crustaceans.

FAMILY HAEMULIDAE
Grunts

Grunts are hard to characterize as most members of the family have one dorsal fin composed of spines and soft rays. The mouth is small, with thick lips, and the upper jaw bone (maxillary) fits into a groove when the mouth is closed. Their grunting sound is made by the rubbing together of the tooth plates in the throat.

The members of this family are mostly tropical, a few occur in warm temperate and brackish waters, and a few even in fresh water. About 175 species are known, 3 from the area covered by this guide.

130. SARGO   *Anisotremus davidsonii*

Identification: This grunt can be identified by the single black bar that extends down the sides from the base of the dorsal fin and passes under the pectoral fin. The 9 to 11 soft-rays in the anal fin distinguishes the sargo from members of the surfperch family (Embiotocidae), which have fewer than 13 anal soft rays. *Size:* Length to 23 inches (58 cm). *Range and Habitat:* Santa Cruz, California, to Magdalena Bay, Baja California Sur, and the upper Gulf of California. Around reefs and kelp beds; to depths of 130 ft (40 m). *Natural History:* Sargo feed on crustaceans, molluscs and bryozoans.

131. SALEMA · · · · · · · *Xenistius californiensis*
Identification: This member of the grunt family can be distinguished by the large eye and the six to eight, horizontal, orange-brown stripes on the sides. *Size:* Length to 10 inches (25 cm). *Range and Habitat:* Monterey Bay, California, to Peru, including the Gulf of California. In aggregations over sandy and rocky shallows and in sheltered bays; in depths from 4 to 35 (1 to 11 m). *Natural History:* This schooling fish spawns in the spring and early summer. The eggs are pelagic.

E. Erikson

FAMILY SCIAENIDAE
Croakers

The long dorsal fin of croakers is usually divided by a notch. It is composed of 7 to 16 spines and the soft rayed part has one spine and many soft rays. Croakers usually have a chin barbel, two spines in the anal fin and the pelvic fins are in the thoracic position. A modified gas bladder is used to make drumming sounds.

The members of the family inhabit near shore tropical, semi-tropical and temperate seas. A few live in estuaries and freshwater. There are about 250 recognized species worldwide, 8 off our coast.

132. BLACK CROAKER
Cheilotrema saturnum
Identification: Black croakers, as the name implies, are blackish in color. They may have coppery tints or even be purplish-bronze. They differ from the other croakers in the lack of a chin whisker and in having 25 to 28 dorsal soft rays. *Size:* Length to 15 inches (38 cm). *Range and Habitat:* Point Conception, California, to Magdalena Bay, Baja California Sur. In rocky crevices and caves during daylight, they come out to feed at night; to depths of 150 ft (46 m). *Natural History:* Black croakers feed on crabs and other small crustaceans. Spawning takes place during spring and summer. The pelagic eggs hatch in only two or three days.

76

133. WHITE CROAKER
Genyonemus lineatus

Identification: White croakers have more spines in the first dorsal fin (12 to 16) than the other croakers on this coast. A small black spot is sometimes present above the base of the pectoral fin. *Size:* Length to 16.3 inches (41 cm). *Range and Habitat:* Barkeley Sound, British Columbia to Magdalena Bay, Baja California Sur; over soft bottoms, inshore from surface to depths of 600 ft (183 m), usually in schools. *Natural History:* White croakers may reach 12 years of age. Spawning takes place from November through April off Southern California and all year off Central California. Females spawn 18 to 24 times each season. Food consists of small fishes, shrimps, crabs, squid, octopus, clams and worms.

134. YELLOWFIN CROAKER
Umbrina roncador

Identification: The yellowfin croaker can be distinguished from the other croakers by the yellowish fins, dark oblique wavy lines on sides of body, small barbel on the chin, and the two spines in the anal fin. *Size:* Length to 20 inches (51 cm). *Range and Habitat:* Point Conception, California, to the Gulf of California. Around kelp beds and over soft bottoms; from surf zone to depths of 150 ft (46 m). *Natural History:* Yellowfin croakers feed on fishes and small invertebrates.

FAMILY KYPHOSIDAE
Sea Chubs

Sea chubs have small mouths, oval bodies and continuous dorsal fins. The ctenoid scales extend onto most of the fins. The members of this family are found in all warm seas.

There are about 40 species worldwide, 4 in the area covered by this guide.

135. OPALEYE *Girella nigricans*

Identification: Opaleye usually have one or more whitish spots on the back, and blue opalescent eyes. *Size:* Length to 26 inches (66 cm). *Range and Habitat:* San Francisco, California, to Cape San Lucas, Baja California Sur. Around shallow reefs and kelp beds; from the intertidal to depths of l00 ft (30 m). *Natural History:* Opaleye feed on a variety of algae and small invertebrates. The larvae are pelagic.

136. ZEBRAPERCH *Hermosilla azurea*

Identification: Zebraperch have 9 or 10 dark vertical bars on their sides, a bright blue spot on the operculum, and a sheath of scales along the base of the dorsal fin. *Size:* Length to 17.4 inches (44 cm). *Range and Habitat:* Klamath River, California, to the Gulf of California. Around kelp beds and off sand and rocky bottoms; from the intertidal to depths of 25 ft (8 m). *Natural History:* These schooling sea chubs also feed on marine algae.

137. BLUE-BRONZE CHUB
Kyphosus analogus

Identification: The blue-bronze chub is similar to the zebraperch in that they have fewer than 15 dorsal soft rays. They lack the vertical bars on the sides; instead there are dark spots on the scales which appear as longitudinal stripes. *Size:* Length to 18 inches (46 cm). *Range and Habitat:* Oceanside, California, to Peru including the Gulf of California; around shallow kelp beds and rocky areas. *Natural History:* Feeds on algae, plankton and invertebrates.

138. HALFMOON *Medialuna californiensis*

Identification: The halfmoon's distinctive half-moon shaped tail, overall grey-blue body, and the sheath of scales covering the soft dorsal and anal fins separate them from all members of the family. *Size:* Length to 19 inches (48 cm). *Range and Habitat:* Vancouver Island, British Columbia, to the Gulf of California. Around reefs and kelp beds; to depths of 130 ft (40 m). *Natural History:* Spawning takes place in the summer, the larvae are pelagic; the young are often associated with floating mats of kelp. Halfmoon feed on algae, but will also ingest bryozoans, sponges and other attached invertebrates.

FAMILY CHAETODONTIDAE
Butterflyfishes

The members of this colorful tropical fish family have discus-shaped, compressed bodies and small protrusible mouths. Butterflyfish are found in all the world's tropical oceans around reefs. Worldwide about 115 species are recognized; 2 species occur in the southern portions of the area covered by this book.

139. SCYTHE BUTTERFLYFISH
Prognathodes falcifer

Identification: The distinctive scythe mark on the sides is the best character for recognition. *Size:* Length to 6 inches (15 cm). *Range and Habitat:* Santa Catalina Island to Galapagos Islands, common around San Benito Islands, Baja California. Around rocky reefs; to depths of 492 ft (150 m). *Natural History:* This deeper water butterflyfish rarely is found shallower than 50 ft (15 m). They are common at Guadalupe and San Benito Islands off Baja California.

FAMILY EMBIOTOCIDAE
Surfperches

Surfperches have continuous dorsal fins, usually with 9 to 11 spines and 19 - 28 soft rays. There are 3 spines by the anal fin, and the caudal fin is forked. All members of the family are viviparous.

The members of this family have only been recorded from the North Pacific; two species occur off Japan and Korea. Twenty-one marine species have been described, 18 off our coast and one freshwater species.

140. KELP SURFPERCH
Brachyistius frenatus
Identification: Kelp surfperch can be separated from shiner surfperch (#141) by their lack of yellow bars on the body and they have only 13 to 16 softrays in the dorsal fin. *Size:* Length to 8.5 inches (22 cm). *Range and Habitat:* Prince Rupert, British Columbia, to Turtle Bay, Baja California Sur. In kelp beds; from surface to depths of 100 ft (31 m). *Natural History:* Kelp surfperch are "cleaners"; they also feed on small crustaceans associated with kelp.

141. SHINER SURFPERCH
Cymatogaster aggregata
Identification: These small, silvery surfperch have three vertical yellow bars on sides. Males during breeding season have black striping which tends to cover the yellow bars. *Size:* Length to 7.6 inches (19.3 cm). *Range and Habitat:* Wrangell, Alaska, to San Quintin Bay, Baja California. Around piers, reefs, kelp beds, and on soft bottoms; from shallow bays to depths of 480 ft (146 m). *Natural History:* These very abundant surfperches feed on small crustaceans. Young are born in the spring and summer; each female releases up to 20 newborn.

142. PILE SURFPERCH *Damalichthys vacca*

Identification: Pile surfperch have very long dorsal soft rays; the longest is about twice the length of the longest dorsal spine. The dark bar on the silvery grey sides is also very distinctive. *Size:* Length to 17.5 inches (44 cm). *Range and Habitat:* Port Wrangell, Alaska to Guadalupe Island, Baja California. Around reefs, kelp beds, and piers; from shallow bays to depths of 150 ft (46 m). *Natural History:* Pileperch feed on a variety of molluscs, crabs and barnacles. Breeding occurs in the summer, gestation period is about 15 months.

143. BLACK SURFPERCH
Embiotoca jacksoni

Identification: This dark surfperch has a patch of enlarged scales between the pectoral fin and pelvic fin, yellow-orange lips, a blue bar at the base of the anal fin, and several dark bars on sides. *Size:* Length to 15.5 inches (39 cm). *Range and Habitat:* Fort Bragg, California, to Point Abreojos, Baja California Sur. Around reefs and kelp beds; from shallow bays to depths of 150 ft (46 m). *Natural History:* The young, about 2 inches (5.1 cm), are born during spring and summer.

144. STRIPED SURFPERCH
Embiotoca lateralis

Identification: Striped surfperch can best be distinguished from the similar rainbow surfperch (#147) by the dusky pelvic fins and 29 to 33 soft rays in the anal fin. *Size:* Length to 15 inches (38 cm). *Range and Habitat:* Wrangell, Alaska, to Point Cabras, Baja California. Around reefs, piers, and kelp beds, from shallow bays to depths to 70 ft (21 m). *Natural History:* As many as 44 juveniles are released by females in the summer. Feed on small crustaceans, worms, mussels and herring eggs.

145. WALLEYE SURFPERCH
Hyperprosopon argenteum

Identification: The walleye surfperch can be separated from the other member of the genus *Hyperprosopon* by the following: If the fish has black tipped pelvic fins and a black edge on tail, it is a walleye surfperch. *Size:* Length to 12 inches (30 cm). *Range and Habitat:* Vancouver Island, British Columbia, to San Benito Islands, Baja California. Around kelp beds and reefs to depths of 60 ft (18 m). *Natural History:* These surfperch feed on small crustaceans. Females release 5 to 12 young.

146. SILVER SURFPERCH
Hyperprosopon ellipticum

Identification: Silver surfperch differ from the walleye and spotfin surfperches by the lack of any dark spots in the dorsal or anal fins, and the pelvic fins are not black tipped. The tail fin is usually pinkish in color. *Size:* Length to 10.5 inches (27 cm). *Range and Habitat:* Schooner Cove, Vancouver Island, British Columbia, to Rio San Vincente, Baja California; in surf and over sand and around rocks and piers to depths of 360 ft (110 m).

147. RAINBOW SURFPERCH
Hypsurus caryi

Identification: The rainbow surfperch has bright blue and red-orange pelvic fins and only 20 to 24 anal soft rays. These characters and the reddish vertical bars on the sides distinguish it from the striped surfperch (#144). *Size:* Length to 12 inches (30 cm). *Range and Habitat:* Cape Mendocino, California, to San Martin Island, Baja California. Around reefs, piers, and kelp beds; from shallow bays to depths of 130 ft (40 m).

148. REEF SURFPERCH
Micrometrus aurora

Identification: Reef surfperch are smaller than most other members of this family. They have a black triangular blotch at the base of the pectoral fin. The scales between the anal and pectoral fins have black edges. *Size:* Length to 7 inches (18 cm). *Range and Habitat:* Tomales Bay, California, to Point Baja, Baja California; from intertidal to depths of 20 ft (6.1 m) around rocky areas. *Natural History:* Feed on algae and small invertebrates.

149. DWARF SURFPERCH
Micrometrus minimus

Identification: Dwarf surfperch, besides being small, have a black triangle at the base of the pectoral fin. Dorsal, anal, and pelvic fins have dark blotches. *Size:* Length to 6.3 inches (16 cm). *Range and Habitat:* Bodega Bay, California, to Cedros Island, Baja California; around shallow, inshore, algae-covered reefs to a maximum depth of 30 ft (9.1 m). *Natural History:* Males are mature at birth, females at about age one. The young are born during the spring and summer; adults feed on crustaceans, molluscs, worms and algae.

150. SHARPNPOSE SURFPERCH
Phanerodon atripes

Identification: The reddish speckles on the scales along the sides and black tipped pelfic fins distinguish the sharpnose surfperch from the white surfperch (#151). *Size:* Length to 11.5 inches (29 cm). *Range and Habitat*: Bodega Bay, California, to San Benito Islands, Baja California. Around deep reefs, kelp beds, and, on occasion, shallow reefs and piers, to depths of 750 ft (229 m). *Natural History:* Sharpnose surfperch occasionally function as "cleaners"; they have been observed picking parasites from molas (#214), blue rockfish (#49), and blacksmith (#154).

151. WHITE SURFPERCH
Phanerodon furcatus

Identification: White surfperch have white pelvic fins, a thin black line at base of the soft-rayed dorsal fin, and the dorsal soft rays are only slightly longer than the longest dorsal spine. *Size:* Length to 13.3 inches (34 cm). *Range and Habitat:* Vancouver, British Columbia, to Point Cabras, Baja California. Around reefs and in kelp beds; from shallow bays to depths of 140 ft (43 m). *Natural History:* One of the most important commercially fished surfperch in California.

152. RUBBERLIP SURFPERCH
Rhacochilus toxotes

Identification: The large fleshy lips of this surfperch have two ventral lobes and the first ray in the soft rayed portion of the dorsal fin is shorter than the third ray; these characters, plus the brassy overtones on the brown body, should confirm identification. *Size:* Length to 18.5 inches (47 cm). *Range and Habitat*: Russian Gulch State Beach, California, to Thurloe Head, Baja California Sur. Around reefs, kelp beds, and piers; from shallow bays to depths of 150 ft (46 m). *Natural History:* Females release young during the summer.

FAMILY POMACENTRIDAE
Damselfishes

The members of this large family of mostly tropical fishes have round to oval compressed bodies, small mouths and the lateral line usually ends below the soft dorsal fin. The continuous dorsal fin has the spiny part longer than the soft rayed part. There are only two anal fin spines. Most damselfishes occur in warm waters, but a few species are found in cooler warm temperate oceans. About 300 species have been described; three species have been recorded from this area.

153. SWALLOWTAIL DAMSELFISH
Azurina hirundo

Identification: This uncommon damselfish has a long, slender, steel-blue body, a deeply forked caudal fin and light pectoral fins. *Size:* Length to 7 inches (18 cm). *Range and Habitat:* Santa Catalina Island, California, to at least Revillagigedo Islands, Mexico; in schools around rocky reefs, from midwater to about 100 ft (30 m). *Natural History:* These attractive damselfish often are found in schools of blacksmith (#154) in midwater apparently feeding on zooplankton.

154. BLACKSMITH   *Chromis punctipinnis*

Identification: This dark blue damselfish has black spots on the body, dorsal fin, and on the tail. *Size:* Length to 12 inches (30 cm). *Range and Habitat*: Monterey, California, to Point San Pablo, Baja California Sur. Around reefs and kelp beds; to depths of 270 ft (82 m). *Natural History:* Blacksmiths are major "customers" of the "cleaners," particularly senoritas (#l58). Young blacksmiths obtain some of their food by picking parasites from other fishes. Adults feed on zooplankton in midwater during the day and return to reef crevices at night.

Juvenile

155. GARIBALDI   *Hypsypops rubicundus*

Identification: The garibaldi's distinctive bright orange color separates it from all other fish in our area. Juveniles have iridescent blue spots on the body. *Size:* Length to 14 inches (36 cm). *Range and Habitat:* Monterey Bay, California, to Magdalena Bay, Baja California Sur, rare north of Point Conception. Around reefs and kelp beds; to depths of 95 ft (29 m). The garibaldi is completely protected by law. *Natural History:* Like most damselfishes, the male garibaldi guards the eggs that are attached to a filamentous red algae. These fish feed on attached invertebrates.

Adult garibaldi

FAMILY SPHYRAENIDAE
Barracudas

These elongate predators have large mouths, and formidable teeth. The cylindrical body has two widely spaced dorsal fins; the anterior dorsal fin usually has five spines. The pelvic fins are in the abdominal position and the caudle fin is forked. Barracudas are found in all the world's tropical seas. Worldwide there are about 20 species, but only one is resident off California.

M. Conlin

156. CALIFORNIA BARRACUDA
Sphyraena argentea
Identification: The California barracuda is distinguished by having numerous large canine teeth and two widely spaced dorsal fins. The caudal fin is yellowish. *Size:* Length to 4.0 ft (1.2 m); weight to 18 lbs (8 kg). *Range and Habitat:* Prince William Sound, Alaska, to Cape San Lucas, Baja California Sur; pelagic, to depths of 60 ft (18 m). *Natural History:* A female may release 500,000 pelagic eggs. Barracudas feed on other fishes.

FAMILY LABRIDAE
Wrasses

The members of this large, tropical fish family usually have protruding upper and lower jaw teeth. There is one long dorsal fin with weak spines in front. Most wrasses are sequential hermaphrodites.

Wrasses occur worldwide in warm waters, with a few species preferring temperate seas. Some species bury themselves in sand or gravel at night. There are about 500 species worldwide; four of these occur in the area covered by this guide.

157. ROCK WRASSE
Halichoeres semicinctus

Identification: Rock wrasse have a lateral line that has an abrupt arch beneath the posterior portion of the dorsal fin. Males have a dark blue bar near the base of the pectoral fin. Adults have red eyes. Juveniles have dark stripes on sides. *Size:* Length to 15 inches (38 cm). *Range and Habitat:* Point Conception, California, to Gulf of California. Around reefs and in kelp beds; to depths of 78 ft (24 m). *Natural History:* Rock wrasse are hermaphroditic. Females change into males at about 5 years of age. Spawning occurs in the summer. Rock wrasse feed on small invertebrates such as crustaceans and molluscs.

Juvenile

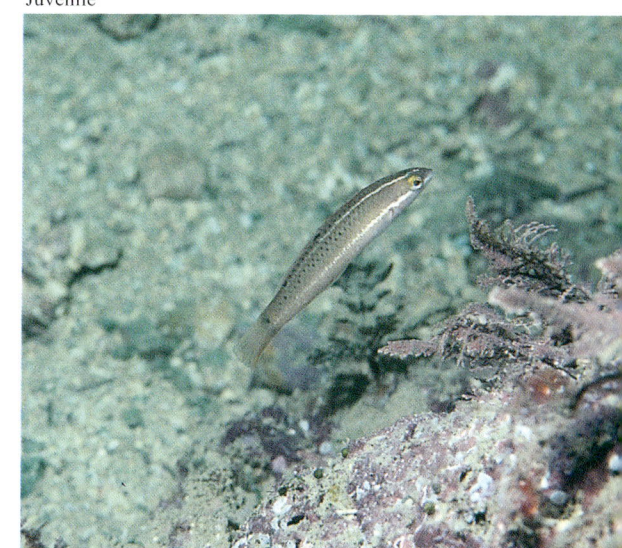

Female

Male rock wrasse

Juvenile

158. SEÑORITA   *Oxyjulis californica*

Identification: The only dusky orange, cigar-shaped wrasse with large scales and a black spot on the tail fin in our area. *Size:* Length to 10 inches (25 cm). *Range and Habitat:* Salt Point, Sonoma County, California, to Cedros Island, Baja California, Mexico. Around reefs and in kelp beds; to depth of 331 ft (l0l m). *Natural History:* The most common "cleaner" in California. Señoritas also feed on zooplankton in midwater beneath kelp canopy. Buries itself in the sand at night.

159. CALIFORNIA SHEEPHEAD
Semicossyphus pulcher

Identification: Both sexes of California sheephead have large doglike teeth and white chins. Juveniles have seven black blotches, of which five are visible from the side on the fins and base of tail. *Size:* Length to 3 ft (9l cm). *Range and Habitat:* Monterey to Cape San Lucas, Baja California Sur, Mexico, and an isolated population in the northern Gulf of California. Around reefs and in kelp beds; to depths of 289 ft (88 m). *Natural History:* Sheephead are hermaphroditic; when sexually mature they become females, but after a few years almost all will become males for the remainder of their lives. These wrasse feed on sea urchins, molluscs, lobsters and crabs.

Female California Sheephead
Male California Sheephead

Cordell Expeditions

160. INDIGO WRASSE *Pseudojulis* sp.

Identification: This undescribed wrasse is distinguished by the iridescent indigo blue stripe at the base of the dorsal fin that extends to the caudal fin in females. Males have yellow bodies with a black bar under the center of the dorsal fin. *Size:* Length to about 5 inches (13 cm). *Habitat:* Around reefs, to depths of at least 60 ft (18 cm). *Range:* Isla Guadalupe, Baja California, to the Islas Revillagigedo, Mexico.

FAMILY BATHYMASTERIDAE
Ronquils

Ronquils are elongate fishes with very long dorsal and anal fins composed almost entirely of soft rays. The pelvic fins are in the thoracic position.

Members of this family occur only in the North Pacific. They are bottom dwellers. There are about 9 species in our area.

Plain color phase

161. ALASKA RONQUIL
Bathymaster caeruleofasciatus

Identification: The Alaskan ronquil has only three or four unbranched soft rays on the first part of the dorsal fin. In addition, the Alaskan ronquil differs from other members of the genus *Bathymaster* by having scales on the inner rays of the pelvic fin and on the caudal fin for more than 1/2 of its length; the maxillary extends to or past the posterior edge of the eye. *Size:* Length to about 12 inches (30 cm). *Range and Habitat:* Sea of Okhotsk and Bering Sea to Queen Charlotte Islands, British Columbia, Canada, on rocky bottoms in crevices and caves; to depths of about 100 ft (31 m).

162. STRIPEFIN RONQUIL
Rathbunnella alleni

Identification: The fin rays are pigmented. Body color varies with age and sex. This ronquil and the bluebanded ronquil (#163) require microscopic examination to differentiate. If observed off central California, it is the stripefin ronquil, but those observed off southern California are bluebanded ronquils. *Size:* Length to about 8 inches (20 cm). *Range and Habitat:* This ronquil occurs off central California, from Point Conception to San Francisco on sandy and rocky bottoms, in depths of 50 to about 300 ft (15 to 92 m).

Spotted color phase
M. Chamberlain

163. BLUEBANDED RONQUIL
Rathbunnella hypoplecta

Identification: This ronquil is very similar to #l62, but the males have large dark blotches on the sides. The colors vary with sex and age. This is the only ronquil that occurs in southern California and northern Baja California. *Size:* Length to about 8 inches (20 cm). *Range and Habitat:* Point Conception south to central Baja California, on sand and rocky bottoms, in depths of about 80 to 300 ft (24 to 92 m). *Natural History:* The male guards the eggs. Females may produce more than one batch of eggs during the year.

164. NORTHERN RONQUIL
Ronquilus jordani

Identification: The first 20 to 30 soft rays in the dorsal fin are unbranched in this ronquil; they also have orange stripes below the eye and on the lower posterior portion of the body. Size: Length to 7 inches (18 cm). *Range and Habitat:* Bering Sea and Amchitka Island to Monterey Bay, California. On sand and rocky substrate; in depths from 60 to 917 ft (18 to 275 m). This ronquil feeds on crustaceans, clam larvae and worms.

91

FAMILY STICHAEIDAE
Pricklebacks

Pricklebacks are eel-like fishes with small mouths. The long dorsal fin is sometimes joined to the caudal fin; all rays are spiny except in a few species. The small pelvic fins when present are thoracic and have one spine. The long anal fin has one to five small spines. The very small scales are often buried or absent on part of the body. The members of this family are restricted to the cold waters of the Northern Hemisphere. There are about 60 species; 23 occur in the area covered by this guide.

G. Jensen

165. SLENDER COCKSCOMB
Anoplarchus insignis

Identification: The fleshy crest on the top of the head and lack of pelvic fins are distinctive. *Size:* Length to 4.75 inches (12 cm). *Range and Habitat:* Aleutian Islands to Arena Cove, Mendocino County, California; among shallow subtidal rocks to about 100 ft (30 m).

166. MONKEYFACE PRICKLEBACK
Cebidichthys violaceus

Identification: The monkeyface prickleback has a high, fleshy ridge with two bumps on top of the head and two dark bars radiating posteriorly from the eyes. They also lack pelvic fins. *Size:* Length to 30 inches (76 cm). *Range and Habitat:* Brookings, Oregon, to San Quintin Bay, Baja California. In crevices and holes in rocky areas; to depths of 80 ft (24 m). Monkeyface pricklebacks feed on a variety of crustaceans and algae.

167. DECORATED WARBONNET
Chirolophis decoratus

Identification: There is a large cirrus in front of each eye, dense cirri on the head and anterior dorsal fin spines. Pelvic fins present. *Size:* Length to 16.5 inches (42 cm). *Range and Habitat:* Bering Sea to Humboldt Bay, California; on rocky substrate, subtidal depths to 300 ft (92 m). *Natural History:* These pricklebacks feed on shrimp and other crustaceans.

G. Jensen
G. Jensen

168. MOSSHEAD WARBONNET
Chirolophis nugator

Identification: This distinctive fish has 12 to 13 eye spots or ocelli along the dorsal fin and a dense cluster of small cirri on the head. These characters separate it from the decorated warbonnet, which has a large complex cirrus (the length exceeds the diameter of the eye) in front of each eye and cirri on the first four or five dorsal fin spines. *Size:* Length to 6 inches (15 cm). *Range and Habitat:* Aleutian Islands to San Miguel Island, California; in crevices around rocky areas; to 264 feet (81 m).

R. Borema

169. SIX SPOT PRICKLEBACK
Kasatkia seigeli

Identification: The five to six ocelli on the dorsal fin and large pectoral fin are distinctive. *Size:* Length to about 5.5 inches (14 cm). *Range and Habitat:* Mendocino to Diablo Cove, California; among rocks to depths of about 85 ft (26 m). *Natural History:* This species is considered rare, probably because of its cryptic habits.

170. SNAKE PRICKLEBACK
Lumpenus sagitta

Identification: The long head is almost 1/10th of total length. There is one spine in the anal fin and dark spots at the dorsal fin base. *Size:* Length to 20 inches (51 cm). *Range and Habitat:* Sea of Japan and Bering Sea to Humboldt Bay, California; on soft bottoms in bays and offshore to about 680 ft (207 m). *Natural History:* Young snake pricklebacks feed on copepods; larger fish apparently feed on worms as these are used for bait by anglers when this fish is caught.

G. Jensen
R. Borema

171. MASKED PRICKLEBACK
Ernogrammus walkeri

Identification: The "mask" formed by a dark stripe that runs from the snout through the eye is very distinctive. *Size:* Length to 12.75 inches (32 cm). *Range and Habitat:* Monterey Bay to San Miguel Island, California; on rocky bottoms from intertidal to 70 ft (21 m). *Natural History:* This cryptic fish is rarely observed, nocturnal.

FAMILY CRYPTACANTHODIDAE
Wrymouths

The dorsal fin of these elongate fishes is composed entirely of stiff spines. The dorsal and anal fins are joined to the caudal fin. There are no pelvic fins. The eyes are set high on the broad, flat head. The members of this family are restricted to the northern hemisphere. Four species are known, two from this area.

172. GIANT WRYMOUTH
Delolepis gigantea

Identification: The brownish color, elongate body and oblique large mouth, with protruding lower jaw, are distinctive. *Size:* Length to at least 46 inches (117 cm). *Range and Habitat:* Bering Sea to Humboldt Bay, California. On soft bottoms, 20 to 420 ft (6.1 to 128 m). *Natural History:* These fearsome looking fish spend most of their time buried in the sand or mud.

N. McDaniel

FAMILY PHOLIDAE
Gunnels

The long, compressed, eel-like bodies have very long dorsal fins, extending from the head to the caudal fin, and composed entirely of spines. The dorsal and anal fins join the caudal fin.

There is no lateral line. Gunnels are found only in the North Pacific and Atlantic oceans. There are about 15 species, of which 7 occur off our coast.

G. Jensen

173. PENPOINT GUNNEL
Apodichthys flavidus

Identification: There is a single spine in the anal fin that is grooved like a pen point. There are no pelvic fins; a dark streak extends down from the eye and occasionally a second dark streak radiates from rear of eye. *Size:* Length to 18 inches (46 cm). *Range and Habitat:* Kodiak Island, Alaska, to Santa Barbara Island Island, California; rocky intertidal and shallow subtidal. *Natural History:* Spawning takes place in the winter. These gunnels feed on small crustaceans and molluscs.

95

174. LONGFIN GUNNEL *Pholis clemensi*

Identification: This gunnel has a very long anal fin which exceeds l/2 of body length. The 15 pale saddles at the base of dorsal fin usually have a dark speck inside. *Size:* Length to 5 inches (13 cm). *Range and Habitat:* Alaska to Arena Cove, California. In rocky areas from 24 to 210 ft (7 to 64 m).

F. Bavendam

175. CRESCENT GUNNEL *Pholis laeta*

Identification: The crescent gunnel has a distinctive series of black crescent shaped marks along the base of the dorsal fin, and the enclosed space is yellow to orange. They have large pectoral fins and very small pelvic fins. *Size:* Length to 10 inches (25 cm). *Range and Habitat:* Bering Sea to Crescent City, California. Intertidal rocky areas to depths of 240 ft (73 m).

G. Jensen

176. SADDLEBACK GUNNEL *Pholis ornata*

Identification: The U-shaped or V-shaped black markings at the base of the dorsal fin and large pectoral fin are distinctive. *Size:* Length to 12 inches (30 cm). *Range and Habitat:* Vancouver Island, British Columbia, to Carmel Bay, California; on soft bottoms, among eelgrass to 120 ft (37 m). *Natural History:* These gunnels feed on a variety of small molluscs and crustaceans. The egg mass is guarded by both male and female.

FAMILY ANARHICHADIDAE
Wolffishes

The members of this small family have eel-like tapering bodies with large heads and a long dorsal fin composed only of spines. The canine teeth are large and in the front of the mouth; the rear of the mouth contains strong molar teeth.

The nine recognized species occur only in the northern hemisphere, only one species on this coast.

177. **WOLF-EEL** *Anarrhichthys ocellatus*
Identification: Wolf-eels lack pelvic fins and possess large, strong, canine and molar teeth. *Size:* Length to 6.7 ft (2 m). *Range and Habitat:* Sea of Japan and Kodiak Island to Papalote Bay, Baja California. In and around reefs with crevices and caves; to depths of 738 ft (225 m). *Natural History:* Wolf-eels feed on crabs, urchins, and other hard shelled invertebrates. Both male and female guard the eggs and may mate for life.

Juvenile

Female

Male

FAMILY CLINIDAE
Kelpfishes and Fringeheads

The long dorsal fin of the members of this family extends from the rear of the head to just in front of the caudal fin. These small fish usually have scales, and the dorsal fin has more spines than soft rays. The pelvic fins are thoracic.

Clinids are usually carnivorous and occur in temperate and tropical waters. There are about 200 species recognized worldwide; eleven species occur in the area covered by this guide.

178. ISLAND KELPFISH *Alloclinus holderi*

Identification: Island kelpfish have very long pectoral fins, extending at least to the origin of the anal fin. The lateral line descends abruptly at about mid-body. *Size:* Length to 4 inches (10 cm). *Range and Habitat:* Santa Cruz Island, California, to Point San Pablo, Baja California Sur. Around rocky areas; to depths of 162 ft (50 m). *Natural History:* The most common member of the family observed by divers off the southern Channel Islands of California.

179. ORANGETHROAT PIKEBLENNY
Chaenopsis alepidota

Identification: Lack of scales and lateral lines, and the elongate body and large mouth are distinctive. *Size:* Length to 6 inches (15 cm). *Range and Habitat:* Anacapa Island, California, to Banderas Bay, Jalisco, Mexico, including the Gulf of California. Pikeblennies live in worm tubes; usually on sandy bottoms, in depths to 75 ft (23 m).

180. DEEPWATER KELPFISH
Cryptotrema corallinum

Identification: Differs from the island kelpfish by having its lateral line high on the sides for about 66 percent of the body length. *Size:* Length to 5 inches (13 cm). *Range and Habitat:* Santa Cruz Island, California to San Quintin Bay, Baja California; in depths of 78 to 300 ft (24 to 9l m).

181. KELPFISH   *Gibbonsia* spp.

Identification: There are four species of *Gibbonsia* in our area. They are difficult to separate without the use of a microscope: If the dorsal soft-rays are evenly spaced it is the striped kelpfish, *G. metzi;* if the posterior dorsal soft rays have wider spacing than the anterior rays and there are scales on the caudal fin, it is the spotted kelpfish, *G. elegans;* if there are no scales on the caudal peduncle or tail, it is the crevice kelpfish, *G. montereyensis;* if there are no scales on the caudal fin but there are scales on the caudal peduncle, it is the scarlet kelpfish, *G. erythra. Size: G. metzi, G. elegans, G. montereyensis,* and *G. erythra:* lengths to 9.5, 6.2, 4.5, and 6.0 inches respectively (24, 16, 11 and 15 cm). *Range and Habitat: G. metzi:* Vancouver Island, British Columbia, Canada, to Point Rompiente, Baja California Sur; *G. elegans:* Point Piedras Blancas, California to Magdalena Bay, Baja California Sur; *G. montereyensis:* British Columbia to Rio Santo Tomas, Baja California; *G. erythra:* Santa Cruz Island, California to Point Banda, Baja California. All on reefs with algae or kelp; to depths of 30, 185, 70, 120 ft (9, 57,2l, and 37 m), respectively.

182. GIANT KELPFISH
Heterostichus rostratus

Identification: The giant kelpfish is the only member of the family in our area with a forked tail. The color is highly variable and usually matches the kelp or algae in the vicinity. *Size:* Length to 24 inches (61 cm). *Range and Habitat:* British Columbia to Cape San Lucas, Baja California. Around algae and kelp; to depths of 132 ft (40 m).

G. Jensen

183. SARCASTIC FRINGEHEAD
Neoclinus blanchardi

Identification: Sarcastic fringeheads have two ocelli in the dorsal fin, one between the first and second spines and the other between the fifth and ninth spines; also the maxillary extends almost to the back edge of the gill cover. None of the cirri over the eyes is larger than the diameter of the eye. *Size:* Length to 12 inches (30 cm). *Range and Habitat:* San Francisco, California, to Cedros Island, Baja California. In holes and crevices on soft and rocky bottoms; in depths from 10 to 200 ft (3-6l m). *Natural History:* Male guards eggs. This ambush predator probably feeds on small fishes, crustaceans and other invertebrates that come within range of its large mouth.

184. YELLOWFIN FRINGEHEAD
Neoclinus stephensae

Identification: This fringehead lacks ocelli in the dorsal fin and has three pairs of large branches cirri above eyes. *Size:* Length to 4 inches (10 cm). *Range and Habitat:* Monterey Bay, California, to Pt. San Hipolito, Baja California Sur. *Natural History:* Yellowfin fringeheads are nearly always observed in holes in rocks or sandstone, with only the head sticking out; in depths of 10 to 90 ft (3 to 27 m).

185. ONESPOT FRINGEHEAD
Neoclinus uninotatus

Identification: The largest cirrus above each eye is larger than the diameter of the eye and the single ocellus in the anterior dorsal fin are good characters to distinguish this fringehead. *Size:* Length to 9.75 inches (25 cm). *Range and Habitat:* Bodega Bay to San Diego, California. In holes and crevices on soft and rocky bottoms; in depths from 10 to 90 ft (3 - 27 m). *Natural History:* Fringeheads are very territorial and will attack most intruders near their home. Males and females guard the eggs after their April through June spawning. This fringehead feeds on a variety of crustaceans.

FAMILY BLENNIIDAE
Combtooth Blennies

Blennies lack scales and usually have cirri above the eyes. The name of the family is derived from the close-set row of incisor-like teeth in the jaws that resemble a comb. The pelvic fins have one hidden spine and 2 to 4 soft rays. The origin of the dorsal fin is in front of the pectoral fins and the caudal fin rays are usually branched.

Most members of the family live in tropical waters, but a few live in colder temperate oceans and a few live in fresh water. There are only three, of the 300 known species, that occur off our coast.

186. BAY BLENNY *Hypsoblennius gentilis*
Identification: Bay blennies have a serrated flap (cirrus) above each eye that is not divided or branched at its base. *Size:* Length to 5.8 inches (15 cm). *Range and Habitat:* Monterey to Gulf of California. In crevices around reefs and pier pilings in bays; to depths of 80 ft (24 m). *Natural History:* Bay blennies feed on a variety of small invertebrates and algae.

FAMILY GOBIIDAE
Gobies

Gobies have pelvic fins that are usually united to form a disc or suction cup. There are two dorsal fins; the anterior fin is composed of spines and the posterior fin is made up of soft rays, or occasionally one spine and the rest soft rays.

The lateral line is not discernable. Family members are found in both tropical and temperate seas, but there are more tropical species than temperate. Some occur in fresh water. Of the estimated 2000 species, there are at least 14 known from this coast.

187. BLACKEYE GOBY
Coryphopterus nicholsii

Identification: Blackeye gobies have an iridescent blue spot beneath each eye, long pelvic fins that reach the anus, and a black area on outer edge of the first dorsal fin. *Size:* Length to 6 inches (15 cm). *Range and Habitat:* Queen Charlotte Islands, British Columbia, to Point Rompiente, Baja California Sur, Mexico. On sand, mud, and rock bottoms; intertidal to 420 ft (126 m). *Natural History:* Spawning occurs from April to October. Male cleans area for the eggs then attracts female by rising off bottom and displaying black pelvic fins. The male guards the nest. These gobies feed on molluscs and crustaceans.

188. BAY GOBY   *Lepidogobius lepidus*

Identification: The first dorsal fin has a black edge and there are usually elongate blotches on the sides. The distance between the dorsal fins is very wide. *Size:* Length to 4 inches (10 cm). *Range and Habitat:* Welcome Harbor, British Columbia, Canada, to Cedros Island, Baja California, Mexico; on soft bottoms, usually around or in burrows constructed by other animals; intertidal to 660 ft (202 m).

189.   BLUEBANDED GOBY
Lythrypnus dalli

Identification: This bright red fish has two to six bright blue vertical bands on the body and 12 to 14 soft rays in the anal fin. *Size:* Length to 2.5 inches (6.4 cm). *Range and Habitat:* Monterey, California, to Gulf of California, Mexico, in and around crevices on rocky substrate; to depths of 250 ft (76 m). *Natural History:* These attractive gobies feed on small crustaceans; the male guards the eggs that are deposited in empty shells.

190.   ZEBRA GOBY   *Lythrypnus zebra*

Identification: The zebra goby's body is more orange than red. It has 12 to 16 vertical blue bands and only 9 soft rays in the anal fin. *Size:* Length to 2.2 inches (6 cm). *Range and Habitat:* Carmel Bay, California, to Clarion Island, Mexico. In holes and crevices, around rocky reefs; to depths of 318 ft (97 m).

FAMILY SCOMBRIDAE
Mackerels and Tunas

These pelagic, fast moving, schooling fishes have cigar-shaped streamlined bodies, two dorsal fins, and 5 to 10 finlets behind the second dorsal and anal fins. The caudal peduncle has one to three keels.

Mackerels and tunas are found in most of the world's tropical and temperate waters. Most species migrate long distances. Fourteen of the 45 known species occur off our coast.

191. PACIFIC BONITO *Sarda chiliensis*
Identification: Pacific bonito do not have widely spaced dorsal fins. They do have slightly oblique stripes on the back, below the dorsal fin, and 7 to 9 dorsal finlets and 6 to 7 anal finlets. *Size:* Length to 40 inches (102 cm); weight to 12 lbs (5.4 kg.). *Range and Habitat:* Alaska to Chile. Pelagic, usually in large schools. Sometimes enter bays and harbors. *Natural History:* Pacific bonito feed on fishes and squid, and they spawn from January to May.

192. CHUB MACKEREL *Scomber japonicus*
Identification: The chub mackerel has about 30 irregular and almost vertical bars along the back, extending to the head. The two dorsal fins are widely separated and there are four to six dorsal and anal finlets. *Size:* Length to 25 inches (64 cm) and 6.3 lbs (2.9 kg). *Range and Habitat:* TransPacific; on this coast from Alaska to Chile. Pelagic, in large schools; often mixed with jack mackerel and/or Pacific sardines around kelp beds. *Natural History:* Chub mackerel spawn off California from April to July; a female may produce over 1 million eggs. Food consists of a variety of fishes, crustaceans and squids.

FAMILY STROMATEIDAE
Butterfishes

This family contains fishes with rounded heads, compressed, oval bodies and small mouths. The single dorsal fin is long and contains 3 flattened spines. The pelvic fins are absent in all of the species that occur off our coast.

Family members are pelagic and are found worldwide in cold and warm seas. Young fish associate with floating objects. There are about 60 species worldwide; at least four occur in the area covered by this guide.

C. Tribolet

193. MEDUSAFISH *Icichthys lockingtoni*
Identification: Medusafish have soft, compressed bodies, a single long, low dorsal fin, and rounded caudal fins. Pelvic fins are present. Adults are grey to brown, juveniles lack scales and are almost transparent. *Size:* Length to 16 inches (41 cm). *Range and Habitat:* Japan and Gulf of Alaska to central Baja California; pelagic. *Natural History:* These unique fish associate with various species of large jellyfish, such as *Pelagia.* Very young fish are often found in the tunic of pelagic tunicates (salps). Juvenile medusafish feed on jellyfish tenticles and gonads.

194. PACIFIC POMPANO
Peprilus simillimus
Identification: These fish lack pelvic fins. The silvery body is compressed and the head blunt. The caudal fin is deeply forked. *Size:* Length to 11 inches (28 cm). *Range and Habitat:* Queen Charlotte Islands, Brisith Columbia, to Magdalena Bay, Baja California Sur. In depths of 30 to 300 ft (9.1 to 91 m). *Natural History:* Pacific pompano spawn throughout the year. They feed on pelagic crustaceans. Juveniles associate with large jellyfish.

FAMILY BOTHIDAE
Lefteye Flounders

All flatfishes begin larval life with eyes on both sides of the head; the eyes migrate to one side or the other as the larva matures. These flatfishes usually have both eyes on the left side of the body, as adults. There is a single lateral line and no dorsal branch.

Family members have been recorded from tropical and temperate oceans worldwide. There are about 220 recognized species; seven occur in the area covered by this guide.

195. PACIFIC SANDDAB
Citharichthys sordidus

Identification: If the pectoral fin is bent forward, the tip reaches to about mid-eye. The diameter of the lower eye is greater than the length of the snout. Scales large and apparent. *Size:* Length to 16 inches. *Range and Habitat:* Bering Sea and Kiska Island to Cape San Lucas, Baja California Sur, Mexico; on sand and mud bottoms, in depths of 30 to 1,800 (9 to 553 m). *Natural History:* This popular food fish lives to at least age 10 and spawns during July, August and September. Their food consists of shrimp, crabs, worms, squid eggs, octopus and fishes.

196. SPECKLED SANDDAB
Citharichthys stigmaeus

Identification: Differs from the Pacific sanddab (#195) in having a smaller lower eye (about equal to snout length) and a short pectoral fin, less than length of head. The small scales are not readily apparent. *Size:* Length to 6.75 inches (17 cm). *Range and Habitat:* Southeastern Alaska to Cape San Lucas, Baja California Sur, Mexico; on soft bottoms, 10 to 1200 ft (3 to 366 m). *Natural History:* These small flatfish are usually mature at 1 year and live to about the age of 4 years. Spawning takes place from March to September. They feed on small crustaceans and worms.

197. CALIFORNIA HALIBUT
Paralichthys californicus
Identification: The California halibut has an abrupt, high arch of the lateral line over the pectoral fin, a large mouth, and the maxillary extends beyond the eye. *Size:* Length to 5.0 ft (117 cm). Weight to 72 lbs (33 kg). *Range and Habitat:* Quillayute River, Washington, to Magdalena Bay, Baja California Sur, Mexico, and an isolated population in the upper Gulf of California, Mexico. On mud and sand bottoms; shallow water to depths of 600 ft (183 m). *Natural History:* This very popular sport fish feeds on fishes and squids, both on the bottom, as well as in mid-water. Most spawning takes place during winter and spring.

198. FANTAIL SOLE   *Xystreurys liolepis*
Identification: The fantail sole has large, reddish-brown spots on the side, one under the tip of the long pectoral fin and one near the caudal peduncle. The pectoral fin is larger than the head as measured from the snout to the back edge of the gill cover. *Size:* Length to 21 inches (53 cm). *Range and Habitat:* Monterey Bay, California, to Gulf of California. On sand and mud bottoms; in depths of 15 to 260 ft (5 to 79 m). *Natural History:* These uncommon flatfish feed almost entirely on crustaceans.

FAMILY PLEURONECTIDAE
Righteye Flounders

The members of this family usually, but not always, have both eyes on the right side of the body as adults. Many species have a dorsal branch to the lateral line anteriorly that runs back along the dorsal fin base.

These flounders, for the most part, are restricted to cold seas, but a few are found in tropical waters and a few in fresh water. These are about 100 species worldwide; 22 occur in the area covered by this guide.

199. PETRALE SOLE   *Eopsetta jordani*

Identification: This right-eyed sole has a large mouth. The upper jaw extends to below the middle of the eye. Petrale sole also have two rows of small teeth in the upper jaw. *Size:* Length to 27.5 inches (70 cm). *Range and Habitat:* Bering Sea to Los Coronados Islands, Baja California. On sand and mud bottoms from 60 to 1,500 ft (18 to 457 m). *Natural History:* This very important food fish is known to migrate long distances. They spawn in deep water during the winter and spring, and move inshore after spawning. The oldest fish aged was 25 years old. Feed on a variety of fish and crustaceans.

200. REX SOLE   *Errex zachirus*

Identification: The very long pectoral fin on the eyed side (longer than head), small mouth and straight lateral line are distinctive. *Size:* Length to 23.25 inches (59 cm). *Range and Habitat:* Bering Sea to northern Baja California; on soft bottoms, 60 to 2100 ft (18 to 640 m). *Natural History:* This slow-growing flatfish lives to at least 24 years. Spawns during spring.

G. Jensen

201. PACIFIC HALIBUT
Hippoglossus stenolepis

Identification: Pacific halibut have an elongated diamond-shaped body, the eyes are always on the right side, and the lateral line has a high arch over the pectoral fin. In addition, the mouth is not as large as it is in the California halibut and the maxillary reaches only to the anterior edge of the eye. *Size:* Length to 8.8 ft (2.7 m). Weight to 800 lbs (363 kg). *Range and Habitat:* Sea of Japan and Bering Sea to Santa Rosa Island, California. On sand and mud bottoms; in depths of 20 to 3,657 ft (6 to 1,097 m). *Natural History:* This very important commercial flatfish feeds on fish, crabs, clams and squid. Spawning takes place during the winter. Females are sexually mature at age 12.

107

202. DIAMOND TURBOT
Hypsopsetta guttulata

Identification: The diamond-shaped body with light blue spots and the white underside with lemon-yellow coloring near the mouth and margin of the head are the best characters for identification. *Size:* Length to 18 inches (46 cm). *Range and Habitat:* Cape Mendocino, California, to Magdalena Bay, Baja California Sur, and an isolated population in upper Gulf of California, Mexico. On mud and sand bottoms; in depths of 5 to 150 ft (2 to 46 m). *Natural History:* Females are mature at age two or three and spawn during the spring and summer. Food consists of worms, clams and shrimp.

203. ROCK SOLE   *Pleuronectes bilineata*

Identification: The rock sole has a dorsal fin with an abrupt high arch over the pectoral fin, and a branch of the lateral line that extends toward the tail, and rough scales. *Size:* Length to 23.5 inches (60 cm). *Range and Habitat:* Sea of Japan and Bering Sea to Tanner Bank, California. On rocky and soft bottoms; in depths to 1,200 ft (366 m). *Natural History:* Spawning takes place in Washington from February to April, females are mature at age 4 and reach at least 22 years in age. Rock sole feed on mollusc siphons, polychaetes, shrimps, crabs and brittle stars.

G. Jensen

204. ENGLISH SOLE   *Pleuronectes vetulus*

Identification: The English sole has a pointed head and the lateral line lacks a high arch over the pectoral fin. The edge of one eye is visible from the blind side. *Size:* Length to 22.5 inches (57 cm). *Range and Habitat:* Bering Sea and Aleutian Islands, Alaska to San Cristobal Bay, Baja California Sur, Mexico. On sand and mud bottoms; from shallow bays to depths of 1,833 ft (550 m). *Natural History:* Very important commercial species. Spawns during late winter and early spring. This migrating flatfish feeds on clams, worms, crabs, shrimps and brittle stars.

205. **SLENDER SOLE** *Lyopsetta exilis*

Identification: The upper eye is located at the midline and visible from the blind side. The lateral line is almost straight. *Size:* Length to 13.75 inches (35 cm). *Range and Habitat:* Southeastern Alaska to Cedros Island, Baja California, Mexico, on soft and rocky bottoms, 60 to 1,680 ft. (18 to 512 m). *Natural History:* These slender flatfish spawn in April.

G. Jensen

206. **DOVER SOLE** *Microstomus pacificus*

Identification: These right-eyed sole have very small mouths and short gill openings. The upper end of the gill openings do not extend beyond the upper insertion of the pectoral fin. The lateral line is nearly straight. *Size:* Length to 30 inches (76 cm). *Range and Habitat:* Bering Sea to San Cristobal Bay, Baja California; on mud bottoms from 60 to 3,450 ft (18 to 1,052 m). *Natural History:* This very important commercial species spawns in the winter and the pelagic larvae do not leave the surface waters for several months. Dover sole feed on burrowing invertebrates.

207. **STARRY FLOUNDER**
Platichthys stellatus

Identification: The eyes of the adult starry flounder can be either on the right or left side. They have dark bars on the dorsal and anal fins and very rough scales on the eyed side. *Size:* Length to 3.0 ft (91 cm); weight to 20 lbs (9.1 kg). *Range and Habitat:* Sea of Japan and Arctic Alaska to Santa Barbara, California. On soft bottoms; in depths of 2 to 900 ft (1 to 274 m). *Natural History:* Starry flounders are often found in brackish as well as fresh water. Spawning takes place in the spring; a large female may produce 11 million pelagic eggs. Food consists of clams, worms, crabs, sand dollars, brittle stars and fish.

208. C-O TURBOT *Pleuronichthys coenosus*

Identification: C-O turbots have only five or six dorsal rays on the blind side, and two distinctive marks on the tail: the anterior mark in the form of a half-moon, the posterior mark in the form of a large dark blotch. *Size:* Length to 14 inches (36 cm). *Range and Habitat:* Southeastern Alaska to Cape Colnett, Baja California. On rocky and soft bottoms; in depths to 1,150 ft (350 m). *Natural History:* This is one of the most common flatfish observed by divers in Southern California. The eggs are pelagic and hatch in about 12 days.

209. CURLFIN TURBOT
Pleuronichthys decurrens

Identification: The best character to look for is the nine or more anterior dorsal rays that extend onto the blind side; the first ray is located below a line drawn between the upper corner of the mouth and the base of the pectoral fin. *Size:* Length to 14.5 inches (37 cm). *Range and Habitat:* North-west Alaska to Cedros Island, Baja California. On sand and mud bottoms; in depths of 25 to 1,746 ft (7.6 to 532 m).

210. HORNYHEAD TURBOT
Pleuronichthys verticalis

Identification: This right-eyed turbot has an oval body shape, small mouth, and the first four to six rays of the dorsal fin are on the blind side. They have a long ridge between the eyes, with a sharp spine at the rear, and usually a spine at front. *Size:* Length to 14.5 inches (37 cm). *Range and Habitat:* Point Reyes, California, to southern Baja California, Mexico and the Gulf of California; on soft bottoms from 30 to 660 ft (9 to 201 m).

211. SAND SOLE
Psettichthys melanostictus

Identification: The sand sole has a large mouth and the first four or five dorsal rays that are elongated and free from the membrane that connects the fin rays. *Size:* Length to 24.7 inches (63 cm). *Range and Habitat:* Bering Sea to Redondo Beach, California. On sand and mud bottoms; in depths from 5 to about 1,083 ft (2 to 325 m).

FAMILY CYNOGLOSSIDAE
Tonguefishes

These elongate left-eyed flatfishes have pointed caudal fins that are joined to the dorsal and anal fins. The eye and mouth are small and the snout projects beyond the mouth. Lateral line absent in some species. Tonguefishes lack pectoral fins.

Family members occur for the most part in tropical waters with a few species in temperate oceans. The family contains about 140 species, but only one species off our coast.

212. CALIFORNIA TONGUEFISH
Symphurus atricauda

Identification: These unusual flatfish lack a lateral line and the pelvic fins are on the eyed side. *Size:* Length to 8.25 inches (21 cm). *Range and Habitat:* Yaquina Bay, Oregon, to Panama, on soft bottoms, 5 to 660 ft (1.5 to 201 m). *Natural History:* These flatfish spawn from June through September. They feed on crustaceans and worms.

G. Jensen

FAMILY BALISTIDAE
Triggerfishes

Triggerfishes have deep, compressed bodies. The first dorsal fin is composed of two to three spines. The first spine can be locked into the upright position by a "trigger" mechanism. The mouth and gill slits are small. Most species lack pelvic fins.

This family is composed mainly of tropical species, although a few venture into warm temperate waters. There are about 120 species; three species occur off our coast, particularly during warm water periods (i.e. El Niño conditions).

213. FINESCALE TRIGGERFISH
Balistes polylepis

Identification: Finescale triggerfish have the characteristic triggerfish shape, with a small gill slit. There are three spines in the first dorsal fin. *Size:* Length to 2.5 ft (76 cm). *Range and Habitat:* Point St. George, Del Norte County, California, to Gulf of California, Mexico and Chile. Around reefs as well as over sandy bottoms from shallow inshore areas to depths of 1,680 ft (512 m). *Natural History:* This triggerfish can often be found "sleeping" at night, laying on its side like a "dead" fish. Food consists of molluscs, sea urchins, crustaceans and worms.

FAMILY MOLIDAE
Molas

The members of this small oceanic family have distinctively shaped bodies; the rear of the body appears to have been cut off. This effect is due to the caudal fin which has been reduced to a leathery flap with a scalloped rear edge. The fish also have small mouths and reduced gill openings. The long dorsal and anal fins have a short base. There are no pelvic fins.

Molas are pelagic and are found in all of the world's temperate and tropical oceans. There are two species that occur off our coast.

214. COMMON MOLA   *Mola mola*

Identification: The small mouth, lack of a distinct tail fin, body shape, and elongated dorsal and anal fins are very distinctive. *Size:* Estimated length to 13.1 ft (4 m); estimated weight to 3,300 lbs (1,500 kg). *Range and Habitat:* Warm and temperate seas of the world; on our coast north to British Columbia. Pelagic. *Natural History:* Molas feed on jellyfish. They apparently move inshore along the California coast in late summer and fall to be cleaned of external parasites by cleaners such as senorita (#158) and sharpnose surfperch (#150).

M. Chamberlain

BIBLIOGRAPHY

Baxter, J. L. 1960. *Inshore Fishes of California.* 3rd Rev. Ed., Calif. Dept. Fish and Game, Sacramento. 80 p.

Boschung, H., D.K. Caldwell, M.C. Caldwell, D.W. Gotshall, and J.D. Williams. 1983. *The Audubon Society Field Guide to North American Fishes and Dolphins.* Alfred A. Knopf, New York, 864 p.

Castro, J. I. *The Sharks of North American Waters.* Texas A & M Press. College Station, Texas. 180 p.

Eschmeyer, W.N., E.S. Herald, and H. Hammann. 1983. *A Field Guide to Pacific Coast Fishes.* Houghton Mifflin Co., Boston. 336 p.

Fitch, J.E. 1969. *Offshore Fishes of California.* 4th Rev. Ed., Calif. Dept. of Fish and Game, Sacramento. 80 p.

Fitch, J.E., and R.J. Lavenberg. 1968. *Deep-water Teleostean Fishes of California,* Univ. of Calif. Press, Berkeley. 155 p.

_____ 1971. *Marine Food and Game Fishes of California,* Univ. of Calif. Press, Berkeley, 179 p.

_____ 1975. *Tidepool and Nearshore Fishes of California,* Univ. of Calif. Press, Berkeley, 156 p.

Gotshall, D.W. 1998. *Sea of Cortez Marine Animals.* Sea Challengers, Monterey, Calif. 112 p.

Hart, J.L. 1973. *Pacific Fishes of Canada.* Fish. Res. Bd. of Canada, Bull. 180. 740 p.

Lamb, A., and P. Edgell. 1986. *Coastal Fishes of the Pacific Northwest.* Harbour Publishing, British Columbia. 224 p.

Lea, R.N., R.D. Mc Allister and D.A. Ven Tresca 1999. *Biological Aspects of Nearshore Rock fishes of the Genus Sebastes from Central California.* Calif. Dept. of Fish and Game, Fish Bull. 177. 109 p.

Leet, W.S., C.M. Dewees, and C.W. Haugen - Editors. 1992. *California's Living Marine Resources and Their Utilization.* Calif. Sea Grant, Davis, Calif. 257 p.

Miller, D.J., and R.N. Lea. 1976. *Guide to the Coastal Marine Fishes of California.* Calif. Dept. Fish and Game, Fish Bull. 157. 249 p.

Robins, C.R., R.M. Bailey, C.E. Bond, J.R. Brooker, E.A. Lachner, R.N. Lea and W.B. Scott. 1991. *Common and Scientific Names of Fishes from the United States and Canada.* 5th Ed. American Fisheries Society, Bethesda, Maryland. 183 p.

Thompson, D.A., L.T. Findley, and A.N. Kerstitch. 2000. *Reef Fishes of the Sea of Cortez.* Revised Ed. Univ. of Arizona Press, Tucson. 302 p.

INDEX TO COMMON NAMES

INDEX TO COMMON NAMES

INDEX TO SCIENTIFIC NAMES

COUNTY LIBRARY
TILLAMOOK, ORE.